THE RELIGION OF THE GREEKS
AND ROMANS

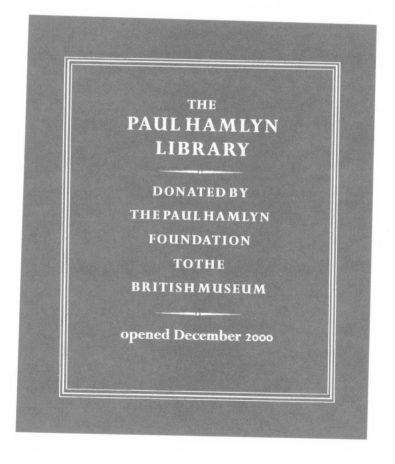

THE RELIGION OF
THE GREEKS
AND ROMANS

C. KERENYI

with 124 monochrome plates

London
THAMES AND HUDSON

Translated by Christopher Holme

© Thames and Hudson 1962
Text printed in Great Britain by
Western Printing Services Ltd Bristol
Plates printed by Hazell Watson and Viney Ltd Aylesbury

CONTENTS

NOTE ON THE PLATES

THE SURVIVING MATERIAL from which our knowledge of ancient religion is derived is both literary and visual. Both are abundant, and archaeology and scholarship in our time have made important additions to both. Thus a selection of pictures, to represent this abundance of visual material as an accompaniment to the text, is an essential part of the plan of this book. These illustrations do not, except in some special cases, refer directly to passages in the text, but are intended to support it with a background of actuality.

The idea of religious style, which is the basis of the approach to ancient religion here adopted, makes particular demands on the illustrator. The elucidation of words and concepts leads us again and again to the world of vision, particularly in the case of Greece, where knowing was seeing, religion was spectacle, and the divine view was the divine act. To concentrate the understanding, in the spirit of the book, on a few salient features, the pictures have been arranged in groups. The division is not hard and fast; each heading applies to the principal illustrations in the group, but not necessarily to all:

> OLYMPIA and the cults of Zeus and Hera
>
> THE ACROPOLIS and the cult of Athena
>
> THE CULTS OF DIONYSUS
>
> DELOS and BRAURON and the cults of Apollo and Artemis
>
> DELPHI and the cult of Delphic Apollo
>
> ROME and the Roman cults.

THE PLATES

THE CULTS OF DIONYSUS

DELOS & BRAURON AND THE CULTS OF APOLLO AND ARTEMIS

The Plates

INTRODUCTION

THIS BOOK SETS OUT TO BE A GUIDE, not to the cult-places of a single deity, such as I sought to provide for those of the divine physician in my *Asklepios*, but to all the cult-places, so to speak, of the Greek and Roman religion. The abundance of surviving material, both monumental and written, demands a more general approach to this task than to the previous one. This abundance, though not without gaps, is great enough to obscure the very thing which the various details of Greek religion have in common; and it is this common characteristic which we need to know before making excursions into different parts of the whole territory, into the domains, that is to say, of the individual deities. In this respect I start from a particular point of view in my treatment of all ancient religion, and should like to say a few words in clarification and justification of it before I embark on any detailed account of the religion of the Greeks and Romans.

The observations which I have made of the two religions from this point of view are here combined with an appropriate selection of pictures. But this is not their first appearance in print. The first version of my observations, which I wrote for an Italian series, bore the title *La Religione Antica nelle sue Linee Fondamentali*. By my use of this term, in English 'fundamentals', I meant to limit myself, but in a positive sense, and I was the first, I think, to introduce such a point of view into the history of religion. The thing to which I wished to direct attention was religious 'Style'. I used the term 'fundamentals' metaphorically, as a simplifying expression for what we call 'Style', something immediately apprehended and spiritually real.

I wrote the foreword to the first Italian edition in Olympia. There in the background was the Altis, the sacred grove of Zeus by the River Alpheus, where there is little more to be seen today than the outlines of the buildings. The reader must be prepared to feel as if he were being shown over a newly excavated sacred precinct. He must accustom his eyes to the discernment of mere outlines, to winning a sense of 'Style' from fragmentary remains. Yet he will be encouraged in this theoretical work by knowing what figures they were which presided over these buildings. And he will get useful help from the chance preservation of some of the statues which used to adorn their summits. We should never forget to keep these figures before our eyes—the portraits of the gods and heroes preserved for us by poetry and art. We should always be ready honestly to examine our thoughts about the past—in this case the religion of the Greeks—to test whether they remain valid in the presence of the products of ancient art.

Walter F. Otto gave the radiant divinities of the Homeric religion their due position in the foreground of his work *The Homeric Gods*. However, he confined himself rather too narrowly to the classical representatives of them in the fifth century B.C., refusing to acknowledge their dark side. I have taken proper account of their more archaic traits in the tales of the gods and heroes offered in my two subsequent volumes, *The Gods of the Greeks* and *The Heroes of the Greeks*, and yet there is no lack in them of references to all that is moving, elevating, or amusing in Greek art. It will not be the task of this book to penetrate too deeply into those earlier times which found their religious expression not in Greek, but in Cretan art. A selection of ancient works of art such as is here offered is the very thing needed to complete a study of the subject of Style in ancient religion.

Strictly speaking, it was no more than a metaphor when I referred, not to 'Style', but to 'fundamentals', foundations, and substructure. My language, however, was not wholly metaphorical when I came to express my conviction that a book about the Style of the Greek and Roman religion should really lay the groundwork for a history of ancient civilisation itself. For the study could be continued either as a history of religion or in the form of a comprehensive account of Greek and Roman civilisation—following the trail laid by Jacob Burckhardt—or even in the form of a history of literature or art. The historical objects which make it possible to write all these histories are *works*, works subject to change as those of religion are, but still *works*—myths and doctrines, rites and institutions, ways of life and communities, pictures and buildings—all of which exhibit a Style.

This aspect of religion, that it must be studied through its *works*, is emphasised by my book *Umgang mit Goettlichen* ('Dealings with the Divine', Goettingen 1955). The reason both for the common Style and for the interconnections of a particular civilisation, in this case the Greek and the Roman, can be stated in one word—a word for which we need not be indebted to the existentialist philosophy—its particular *Existence*. Let me explain more fully what I mean. Christianity is no longer concerned with a '*particular* Existence' as were those religions from which I selected the Greek and the Roman as examples. I chose *two* such religions in order to demonstrate the differences of style between them; these two in particular for obvious historical reasons. They are the nearest to us of any except the Christian and the Jewish religions and they can most naturally be compared with one another. They occurred side by side. The Greek religion influenced the Roman and in late classical times there was certainly also a counter-influence of the Roman religion on the Greek, even though this has not yet been investigated. Yet both remained independent. Moreover the comparison of one with the other can be carried through with a minimum of prejudice, without any preconceived opinions for or against either. Finally, everything which I have said about the two religions can be said about Greek and Roman *Existence*. They occurred side by side, they mutually influenced one another, and both stood in the same relation to ourselves.

How then can we speak of a *particular* Greek or Roman Existence? If this were a purely philosophic question, I should not go into it here. We do not, in speaking of 'Greek' Existence, mean the word in the strictly limited sense of existentialist philosophy. The reality in question is not one that can be immediately apprehended, but one which has to be mediated to us through the works of antiquity. There is no denying that this mediation, especially when the works concerned are works of art, demands an experience without which no scholarly treatment of the reality thus mediated is possible. One approach to Greek Existence, as to something real and characteristic in the variety of material, was Jacob Burckhardt's *History of Greek Civilisation*. Otherwise only rarely has any special attention been given to it, and in the study of Greek religion only by one writer—Ellen Jane Harrison, to whose name I have already paid tribute in the first Italian edition.

She started out from a review of concrete objects, foremost among them the surviving monuments, and tried to penetrate from there to 'life' itself. She called herself a pupil of Nietzsche, Bergson, and the sociologist Durkheim. The biological and sociological functions were in her view the keys to the understanding of the works of Greek religion. She applied the biological point of view in her introductory book, *Prolegomena to the Study of Greek Religion*, the sociological in her second great work, *Themis*. She directed her attention to something *real* and *universal* in the variety of material, but one thing, *quality*, was excluded from her consideration, whether in the sense of *artistic merit* or in that of *style*. The quality of a work of art, when present, was from this point of view a mere addition to the biological and sociological product. And yet 'life', especially community life, is responsible in human existence for products which could never be mistaken for products of mere animal life. The distinction was enshrined in the Greek language, which had two different words for life. *Zoe* was the word for 'mere' life, life uncharacterised, while *bios* meant a characterised existence.

To give only two extreme instances: *zoon* means an unspecified living thing, whereas *bios* is the highly characterised life of a human being, the life which, thus named, created a special category of Greek literature. It was the Greeks who spoke of an *arkhaios bios*—an 'ancient life' (Diodorus Sic. 4.7), for which 'archaic existence' would be an equivalent avoiding the ambiguity of the word 'life' (meaning both *zoe* and *bios*). 'Existence', as the equivalent of *bios*, demands a *characteristic style*. It is unthinkable as a historical reality without Style, for even what we call a lack of Style, or its disintegration, are themselves forms of Style. In the history of science the concept of 'Style' was taken over by Leo Frobenius from art and literature to the study of civilisation, but the works which it was regarded as characterising were always those produced in the course of human Existence. 'Existence' and 'Style' are found together in that reality which the Greeks would call *bios*.

What then is the relation between a religion such as the Greek and the Roman to the *bios*, or characterised Existence, with which it was so intimately bound up in history that it vanished with it? One account of this relation was given by Walter F. Otto in his 1926 lecture 'The Ancient Greek Idea of God' (in the volume *Die Gestalt und das Sein*, 1955, p. 118). 'Wherever religion and culture' he writes 'are still found in their native strength, they are fundamentally one, and more or less to be identified one with another. In such a case religion is not a value additional to cultural goods but the most profound revelation of the peculiar content and essence of a culture. Religion is no doubt directed to the eternal but not simply to the eternal. In its domain of sanctity all the forces and configurations of the cultural community expose their eternal aspect. It comprehends and penetrates the vigorous youth of a culture, as a devout awareness of the unnameable vital cause of its specific will, and of the infinite and eternal reality in which this will has its source and into which it flows. Every culture has its particular will, its own valuations and aims. If this spiritual entity is not aware of its own special character, it may yet discover its depths in the awe of sanctity. All national or tribal communities have been able to tell the world just as much about divine things as they were themselves able to be. Their divine things are nothing else but the infinite cause of their particular genius.'

Otto's way of expressing the close relationship of religion with 'vital cause' is to some extent still derived from the 'philosophy of life' in which Jane Harrison believed—not, it is true, in its utilitarian form. It also has affinities, however, with the cultural theory of Leo Frobenius, and in the sentence 'All national or tribal communities have been able to tell the world just as much about divine things as they were themselves able *to be*' it leads on to the point of view which was to become peculiar to Otto in his later works.

This again has affinities with the fundamental idea of this book, which however in contrast to Otto does not start out from the 'Philosophy of Life' but from the human sense of a *religious attitude* by which we understand man's entering the presence of God or his immediate confrontation of the 'absolute'. From this point of view it was only necessary to apprehend the Greek and Roman form of relationship with the absolute in order to apprehend the Greek and Roman Form in its entirety. Every people exhibits a Form of its own, a Form which makes it that people and no other, in its immediate confrontation of the absolute.

I have here used the word 'absolute' as a description, as non-committal as possible, for everything before which a man stands *religiously*, as before the divine. We have here the original sense of the word 'religious', not referring to a particular religion, but to an attitude of respect, or beyond that, of worship, or more still, a feeling of giddiness on the edge of the abyss, of the Nihil, or 'nothingness'. This attitude may refer either to a god, who will be addressed as 'thou', or to the festal reality of the world—a godly world or a world full of gods—or even to the Nihil in a completely godless world, a *kosmos atheos*. It is the situation which lets nothing be hidden and causes everything essential to come clearly to the fore. The outline of a people's religion which emerges from it at the same time characterises its inmost essence, the peculiar culture of the people in question. A new form of the connection between religion and culture came into being with Christianity, and in the far east with Buddhism. In such a case we have a religion which aspires to be the religion of all mankind, concerned with *Existence* pure and simple, while culture remains, as it is likely to do for a long while yet, peculiar to a people, or *gens*, thus forming its *special Existence*. The historian of religion ought to cry out, Tell of your God or gods without naming them, worship them with bodily movements and rites—all that you do will betray a Style, whether you are a Greek or Roman, a Jew, Persian, or Indian.

The religious attitude pure and simple is, in distinction from the attitude of every day, a *festal* attitude, in a primitive community the festal attitude of the whole community. Through it the characterised Existence, the *bios*, is clearly manifested in a definite, concrete action. It is always a 'Here I stand, I cannot do otherwise', or a 'Here I dance, I cannot do otherwise', or a 'Here I sacrifice, I cannot do otherwise'. That is why ancient religion lays claim, not to *truth* in the dogmatic sense, but to being *genuine* and in that sense *true*—like art and its works. It becomes *false* insofar as it moves away from the *bios*, or more exactly, since the *bios* even while maintaining its original style is more changeable than religion and its works, insofar as the *bios* withdraws from it.

The way here indicated of looking at things is no less historical than any which has claimed to be so in the past study of ancient religion. It is neither 'vitalistic' not 'existentialist' but 'biotic'—in the previously given meaning of the word 'bios'. Characterised Existence is within the historian's reach, origins are not. Change and development are found in history only as change in something permanent, in the writing of history only as change in something recognisable. A description must begin at the point where its object becomes recognisable, whether the object really has its beginning there or not. This is all the more necessary with a description concerned entirely with the 'permanent in change'—as Style has been defined by one historian of literature. I have chosen as starting point one very striking characteristic of Greek religion, and refer to it only in passing because I have extensively treated it in other books. That is its mythological aspect, which forms the explicit subject-matter of the two works of mine mentioned at the beginning and has been theoretically investigated in *Introduction to . . .* or *Essays on a Science of Mythology*, published jointly with C. G. Jung, as well as in my *Umgang mit Goettlichen* ('Dealings with the Divine') and in the essay *Work and Myth* in my *Griechische Miniaturen* (Zurich 1957).

'Myth' is substantially 'content', and insofar as it is this it is concerned, like Christianity and Buddhism, with Existence pure and simple. It occurs, however, only as 'mythology', in a definite Form, and is thus always related to a particular Existence. Ought it not to be possible, however, to perceive certain elements of the form which first showed its perfection in the Greek Style even earlier, in another Style, before the Greek Existence completely established itself in another and ultimately shattered it? Such a possibility is at any rate not to be excluded without further ado, and since that earlier Existence has been brought particularly close to us by magnificent works of art, we should not refrain from looking for a starting-point there. Indeed we were only justified and compelled to do so as long as the works of Cretan art were not accompanied by any intelligible word. The words we hear today are actually Greek, and we read in Cretan characters the names of Greek gods.

The enrichment of our knowledge with new material which now forms part of the Greek tradition has contributed, even if only indirectly and not always explicitly, to the enrichment of this book. The idea which it had from the beginning, of preparing a 'Philosophy of Ancient Religion', has not for that reason been abandoned. But if the method chosen is 'biotic', it must take with it a good deal of those forms of experience mediated, as I have said, only by works of art.

CHAPTER I

The Mythological Strain in Greek Religion

I

THE OUTLINES OF A DEFINITE RELIGIOUS ATTITUDE which at the same time correspond to an inner form appear in perfect clarity on the one hand in Homer and Hesiod, and on the other in the Roman ritual. In one we see the Greek, in the other the Roman *Style*. A first glance, however, at the religious monuments of antiquity in art and literature does not at once take in these outlines of ancient religion and ancient humanity. The picture which lives in the memory of the humanistically educated individual of our civilisation is a different one—much more varied and colourful, more attractive, but apparently also more confused.

From near or far we all know this picture; it is the picture of Greek mythology. *Greek*, for it was dominant also in the art and literature of the Romans and through them in the education of modern times, determined as this was by humanism and classicism. How often this gay society of gods has looked down on us from Renaissance walls and ceilings! In such surroundings how can we be deaf to the scholars who warn us that this mythology above all others will surely lead us astray if we try to learn from it about Greek *religion*—to say nothing of Roman religion? It is easy to minimise the difference between the pagan Olympus of the *palazzi* and the Christian heaven of the Baroque churches. For the same Puritan voices which objected to the former might express similar doubts about the latter, asking whether any serious religion could have been practised in such buildings.

Our experience, by contrast, would have been very different, had we had the good fortune to set foot in one of the holy precincts of the ancient religion before it fell into ruins. There, through the mediation of art and mythology, we could have experienced an instantaneous awareness of a picture of the universe—the picture peculiar to the older Greek religion,

B

which one commentator on Plato's myths has described as 'a *temenos*, or precinct, with a forest of statues of prototypes, examples and sureties for the present'.[1] So it already was far back in the archaic period. It had not then, it is true, the idyllic softness and bodily sensuality which it had taken on by Hellenistic times, as when, for instance, in one of the mimes of Herondas, written in the third century B.C., a visitor to the sanctuary of Asclepius on the island of Cos exclaims: 'The child there! The naked child! If I pinch it, I shall leave a visible mark on its body.' None the less, mythology dominated by the human form is so characteristic of Greek religion as we know it that, if at some earlier period it had ever been otherwise, we should have to say that a revolution had subsequently occurred.

The meaning of the Greek word *mythologia* has been taught us by Plato, who as a philosopher has his reserves about it, but in the manner of his master Socrates does himself recount myths, and has left us his reflections on this activity. The word which for us has hardened through centuries of use into a description of a certain material, its collection and treatment, for him meant, literally, 'telling of myths', and this activity was a form of poetic writing. It seems to be distinguished from the song of the poets only by being in prose.[2] On the other hand, *mythologia* is possible also in metrical form.[3] That is how the poets practise it. From his philosophical standpoint Plato takes an equally negative view of the art of poetry and the art of myth-telling. However, by considering 'mythology' in such association with poetry, he demonstrates unwittingly, and so all the more surely, that he has to do with an independent phenomenon of Greek life, one not subject to philosophical definition and limitation.

He reveals just as unwittingly, in every case where he speaks of *mythologia*, a difference between it and poetry. Poetry is, in his usage, as in Greek usage generally, first of all 'making', even though inspired making—*poiesis*. It is only subsequently that it turns into something *made* and therefore existent, the work itself, which is described by the same name. The other activity too, *mythologia*, is so called by analogy with something which went before it, of which it is always regarded as being a continuation. It presupposes, in fact, an older *mythologia*, one in some degree fixed but not yet dead or rigidly prostrate. A man who pronounces the word *poiesis* is not looking back at an archetype but at his own productive activity, which has brought about the work before him. A man who calls his productive activity a *mythologia*, on the other hand, as Plato called his 'Republic' and his 'Laws',[4] is thinking of a quite definite category of works, a category which he believes himself to have inherited from the past and used again.

Following Plato, not in his theoretical thinking, but in his actions and use of language, and in the wake of his experience, we reach a concept of *mythologia* which corresponds to the Greek phenomenon of that name, at least as it existed towards the end of the classical period. Mythology was an art associated with but distinct from poetry. The two arts frequently overlap one another. The presuppositions of mythology were peculiar to itself, and given by its subject matter. For there is a particular subject matter by which the art of mythology is defined, and is in fact simply what we think of when we hear the word 'mythology'—an ancient, traditional mass of material contained in stories, well known and yet capable of further adaptation, stories 'about gods and divine beings and heroes and all that the underworld contains'. Thus Plato describes it.[5] His own *mythologia* moves in this medium, it *is* the movement *of* this medium. The 'mythology' which it offers us is at any rate still alive, fixed but at the same time in motion, capable of transformation. It can be transformed, indeed, to the extreme point at which transformation takes place no longer merely in the subject-matter but, as with the more sophisticated works of art and with the 'final myths' of Plato's dialogues, in the mind of the story-teller himself.

The artists who adorned the temples and whose works were set up in the holy precincts were at first entitled by the content of their creations to be called 'mythologists'. As they became more and more preoccupied with imitation of the human form for its own sake, this ceased to be so. The new development only came about because Greek mythology always preferred human modes of expressing the divine. Mythology in an earlier period was art, in word as in picture. *Mythos* means the content, the thing expressed,[6] but the second component implies *legein*, the telling. Yet if the history of Greek sculpture and painting ever comes to be written not merely formalistically, but also thematically, that is from the point of view of the form which is inseparable from content, then it will be the story of the emergence of an anthropomorphic mythology and the story will have to be carried to the point at which anthropomorphism frees itself from mythology entirely and becomes pure 'humanism'. And even at this stage we shall still feel the necessity of keeping the *divine* in view. The divine may be present simply in a festal *atmosphere*. It gives sense to the idea of perpetuating what is human. One certain instance of this we see in Tarantine terracottas and probably in the Tanagra figurines.

The mythological strain in Greek religion is bound up with anthropomorphism, the preference for the human form. But is this not the case with every mythology, and not the Greek alone? The Greek religion—or the Roman after it—was not the only one which had or assumed a mythological aspect, an aspect which was always and everywhere anthropomorphic. A great exponent in our own time of a religious feeling drawn from the Bible, Martin Buber, gives the reason for this:[7] 'All anthropomorphism is connected with the need to preserve the concreteness of the meeting'—the meeting with God as Buber sees it, or with the divine, the *theion*, if we wish to use the more general term derived from the Greeks. The human form brings the divine nearer to man and is best adapted to giving a plausible account of the meeting. In respect of the mere fact of anthropomorphism there seems to be no difference between the Greek stories of the gods, whether they are accounts of divine appearances—Epiphanies—or purely mythological tales in which only deities occur, and the corresponding descriptions and narratives of the ancient Orient. Both kinds make use of the human form of the gods. What is special about the Greek stories is not their anthropomorphism but their special version of it.

2

Before the Cretan script, in the form in which it was in use also on the mainland, was deciphered, it could already be inferred from Greek heroic mythology that Greek kings were resident in Mycenae, and in the other princely residences round about, in the second half of the second millennium. Now that the texts have been read and found to be in the Greek language, it is known that the Greeks and their gods were present not only on the mainland but even on Crete itself, from about 1500 B.C. onwards. From the citadel of Mycenae in the period between 1400 and 1100 there comes an ivory group, the style of which is not yet distinct from the Cretan. Greater experts will perhaps one day be able to decide whether it is of island or continental manufacture. The subject, however, is unique. It depicts a pair of goddesses with a child which is trying to go from one goddess to the other. Anthropomorphism would here be a minimal, matter-of-course sort of description. The subject is much more than that, it is *human*. The portrayal of a purely human scene, from the women's quarters of the palace, so to speak, at this period and in this art, cannot be paralleled with any other example. Anyone wishing to put such a purely human interpretation on the group would have to produce positive proof of it. On the other hand, a humanity such as this is not foreign to Greek divine mythology. Something that was already familiar to us from the representation of divine children in the Homeric hymns appears here in a piece of concrete evidence five hundred years earlier.

This decisive characteristic, later of such normal occurrence in Greek remains but for which earlier evidence, other than this ivory, is so far lacking, will be apparent to anyone who compares the Mycenaean group with the general run of Cretan ivory and fayence figurines. In the Cretan religion animals, as forms of divine appearance were, it is true, more in the service of the divine than in early Greece, but 'theriomorphism', the cult of gods in animal shape, even in its Egyptian form, was never dominant in that religion. Those elegant figures, in their strict hieratic attitudes, testify with their ceremonial gestures—arms outstretched or raised above their heads —and also by the snakes they carry in their hands, to a belief in divine epiphanies, such as were in fact engraved on rings by Cretan masters. The attitudes are the epiphany attitudes. Whether it is the priestesses who receive the appearing goddess or the goddess who advances to meet the priestesses, as if to say, 'Thus I appear', the gestures are the same. The gestures and attitudes in Cretan art generally are of central importance, but they are always indicative of some festal event or belong to a cult performance, to a festival play. There is here a clear and general difference of Style. It distinguishes the Cretan religion from any which, like the Mycenaean ivory, expresses its meaning through a particular situation such as might occur among human beings.

In Crete, man met godhead in the fashion of a cult which, even in its anthropomorphic form, to say nothing of theriomorphic or other modes of expression, emphasised the distinctness of the divine nature. The new way, on the other hand, contrived, in the Greek fashion, to base the meeting with the gods on their human aspect, like a meeting between man and man, or as if the gods allowed men to see them sometimes wholly in human shape. On this basis the gods, even on the mainland, were worshipped for a long while yet in stern anthropomorphic cult portraits. In order to characterise Greek religion's idea of the gods, the word 'human' must be used in a sense which implies neither the 'humane'—the gods of Greece, especially in the archaic period, often showed themselves as terrible—nor the merely anthropomorphic. The purely human mythology which has become known to later ages principally through Ovid and through mockers and opponents like Lucian and the Church fathers is a later outcome not so much of the religion itself as of a way of looking at things which was specially Greek.

A genuine, original mythology, the art of telling about gods and thus enabling them to be visualised, is not only presupposed but also actually offered us by the group of the two goddesses and the divine child in Mycenae. This carver in ivory was in his own way a *mythologos*. He had no need to name names but took up a tale of gods already known to him, from the telling. One goddess puts her arm round the other, who grasps the embracing hand and looks sympathetically at what is happening, at the child straining away from her lap towards her companion. A tablet from the palace of Pylos names 'two (divine) ladies'—in the closest relationship with one another through the use of the grammatical dual—who receive an offering together with Poseidon. Here are two isolated pieces from a mythological puzzle. We do not know whether the pieces belong together or not, nor, if they do, whether Poseidon is to be regarded as the child or the father of the child, and in this case whether we have to do with the *Despoina*, the Arcadian divine queen, and her mother. This is a warning to us of the difficulty of taking in the mythological pattern at a glance. It is always characteristic of Greek religion and yet for us is never free from gaps. It is thus that the limits of our knowledge are set. Without mythology there is no knowledge about Greek religion, and this knowledge ceases at the point where evidence of the cult is not associated with a myth. The brief text on its own would not even be certain evidence of the existence of a mythology, still less of its specially human quality. This evidence is given by the little work of art.

1 'A humanity such as this is not foreign to Greek mythology' (*see p. 21*)
Ivory group of the divine child watched over by two nurses. Mycenae, about 15th century B.C.
National Museum, Athens

2 'Those elegant
figures, in their strict
hieratic attitudes,
testify with their
cult-like gestures . . .
to a belief in divine
epiphanies' (see p. 21)
*Faience earth-goddess
with snakes, from the
central sanctuary in the
Palace of Knossos,
c. 1600–1580 B.C.
Heraklion Museum*

3 *Bronze statue of Artemis,*
recently found at Piraeus. Piraeus Museum

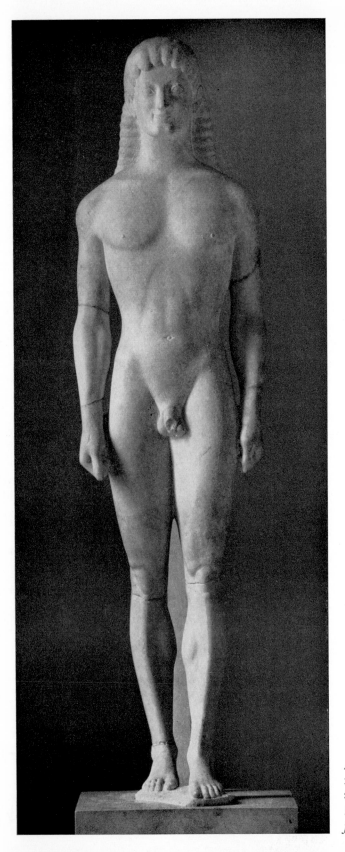

4 'The imitation of Apollo by the young
men can be inferred from the Kouros
statues' (*see p. 30*)
*Standing youth (the so-called Apollo of Tenea),
found at Tenea near Corinth. Glyptothek, Munich*

3

It is Greek mythology we have in mind as example and prototype when the word 'mythology' is mentioned at all. Its humanity, which is more than mere anthropomorphism, is familiar to us. Yet this very humanity was for long a barrier to our understanding of the importance of the mythological strain in Greek religion. This abundance of the merely human seemed to be irreconcilable with a religious aim, whether envisaged in the worship of a deity or in the fulfilment of a wish by supernatural forces. It does indeed go beyond what would be needed merely to preserve the concreteness of the meeting with the divine. If we regard a mythology like the Greek as an essential component of a religion, then we must considerably enlarge our conception of what religion was for the peoples of antiquity.

Greek religion, however, is only a special case of a general phenomenon covered by the term 'mythology', a spiritual activity and literary form which, as we know from Sumerian texts, was already flourishing in Mesopotamia in the third millennium B.C., and in Asia Minor had given rise to the Hurrian and Hittite myths in the second millennium, to say nothing of other territories and cultures which also had their mythologies. The description 'literary' is applicable to this form of spiritual creation, while it still lived, only inasmuch as myths were even at that period written down, certainly not, however, in the sense that they had the character of entertainments. What was merely entertaining was more likely to remain unwritten. Mythology occupies a higher position in the *bios*, the Existence, of a people in which it is still *alive* than poetry, story-telling, or any other art.

This position is accurately described by the anthropologist Bronislaw Malinowski in the light of his discoveries in a Melanesian culture, on the Trobriand Islands, where he came in contact with a mythology in its own lifetime.[8] 'Myth as it exists in a savage community, that is, in its living primitive form, is not merely a story told, but a reality lived. It is not of the nature of fiction, such as we read today in a novel, but it is a living reality, believed to have once happened in primeval times, and continuing ever since to influence the world and human destinies. This myth is to the savage what, to a fully believing Christian, is the Biblical story of Creation, of the Fall, of the Redemption by Christ's Sacrifice on the Cross. As our sacred story lives in our ritual, in our morality, as it governs our faith and controls our conduct, even so does his myth for the savage' (p. 21).

'These stories'—so Malinowski continues his precise account—'live not by idle interest' (this is directed against the notion that myths represent a sort of primitive science, created in answer to intellectual needs) 'not as fictitious or even as true narratives; but are to the natives a statement of a primeval, greater, and more relevant reality, by which the present life, fates, and activities of mankind are determined, the knowledge of which supplies man with the motive for ritual and moral actions, as well as with indications as to how to perform them' (p. 39).

There is both clarity and acuteness in this definition of the relation of the *mythos* to the *bios*, of the myths to the Existence they form. It can be made to yield schematic lines which may sometimes seem somewhat rigid in the light of the historical facts, where these can be ascertained, but which can for that very reason serve for our orientation. In the domain of myth is to be found not ordinary truth but a higher truth, which permits approaches to itself from the domain of *bios*. These approaches are provided by sacred plays, in which man raises himself to the level of the gods, plays too which bring the gods down from their heights. Mythology, indeed, especially Greek mythology, could in some sense be considered as the plays of the gods, in which they approach us. It was because their relationship to the whole of human existence took this dramatic form that the world of gods too was invested among the Greeks with a special humanity.

In the language of the Platonists the plane of myth would have to be called the archetypal, that of the *bios* the ectypal, plane, and their relationship that of the archetypal to the ectypal world. Dogmatic philosophers, and also primitive peoples where they were tied to their social systems, have tended to let this relationship grow rigid, while poets and artists, and those peoples capable of development, have been more ready to give scope to possible ways of bringing the two together. This relationship has been wonderfully realised, for instance, by Thomas Mann. He found the indication of it in the mythological sources to his *Joseph and his Brethren*, and in the novel itself the drama of the passage from one plane to the other has been incomparably worked out. In his commemoration lecture 'Freud and the Future', in 1936, he treated the question theoretically.

'The ancient Ego and its awareness of itself was different from ours, less exclusive, less sharply defined. It was, so to speak, open to rearward, absorbing a great deal of the past in its experience, and repeating it in the present, so that it became "there again". The Spanish philosopher Ortega y Gasset expresses this idea by saying that ancient man, before he does anything, takes a step backwards, like the bullfighter drawing himself back for the death stroke. He looks into the past for a prototype, into which he slips as into a diving-bell before plunging, at the same time protected and disfigured, into the present problem. Thus his life is in a sort of way a revival, a form of "archaising" behaviour. But this life as revival is just what the life in myth is. Alexander walked in the footsteps of Miltiades, and in the case of Caesar his ancient biographers were rightly or wrongly convinced that he intended to imitate Alexander. This "imitation", however, is much more than is conveyed by the word today. It is mythical identification, a procedure which was specially familiar to the ancient world but has retained its efficacy right into modern times and, spiritually speaking, is open to anyone at any time. Attention has often been drawn to the archaic traits in the figure assumed by Napoleon. He regretted that the modern consciousness did not allow him to give himself out as the son of Jupiter-Ammon, as Alexander had done. But we need not doubt that he confounded himself mythically with Alexander at the time of his expedition to the East, and later when he had decided on an empire of the West, he declared, "I *am* Charlemagne". Be it noted that he did not say, "I recall Charlemagne", nor "My position is like Charlemagne's", nor even "I am as Charlemagne", but simply "I *am* he". This is the mythical formula' (p. 33).

The case of Napoleon, treated by Thomas Mann, belongs rather to late antiquity and has its forerunners in the emperor-worship of the ancient Orient and Rome, which, in fact, can only be understood in the light of this possibility of the 'life in myth'. The coarsening process that set in during later classical times grossly affected both art and religion. The emperor cult was associated with the massive style characteristic of this period. Ancient religion no doubt includes the possibility of the 'life in myth', but in definite modes, each of which must be considered separately. One of these modes was certainly the 'quotation', for which Thomas Mann coined the phrase 'life by quotation'. The experience of Sir George Grey is instructive in this context.[9] He was the British administrator who, as

Governor-General of New Zealand, felt the need to collect and write down the myths of Polynesia, in order to be able to deal with the native chieftains on terms of real understanding, since they continually quoted them in their letters and speeches. They lived 'by quotation'. Sir George Grey published these myths in his *Polynesian Mythology and Ancient Traditional History of the New Zealand Race* (1855). Similarly, we too have to learn the ancient mythology when we want to understand the classical authors. A literature so full of mythological quotations must have been preceded by the *life* in myth.

The mythological quotation first occurred in the Existence of the ancient world not, we may be sure, as an exposition in words but as an imitation. All the same the mythical identification was not carried quite so far as in Thomas Mann's account or as it so often was in late classical times. Even where the identification was strongest, it was supposed to be an *imitatio per ludum*, an imitation in play. This exact paraphrase can be inferred from a late author, the Roman satirist Juvenal, who speaks with disapproval of what goes on in one of the secret women's cults (Juvenal 6. 324):

> nil ibi per ludum simulabitur, omnia fient
> ad verum . . .

'Nothing will there be imitated as in play, everything will be done in earnest . . .' As in play, the myth might be quoted in life, and the *bios* thus remained in its correct relation to the myth, with the Romans as with the Greeks.

Even the greatest and most general sacrifice of the Greeks, the sacrifice of oxen, can be viewed as a 'mythological quotation'.[10] It is said to have been an imitation of the 'cheat of Prometheus', who divided the portions of the sacrificial feast so unequally between gods and men that the men came off better. Entire ages of man were shaped as 'quotations'. From their ninth year till their marriage, the Athenian girls, as little she-bears in Brauron, used to imitate in play the goddess Artemis.[11] The imitation of Apollo by the young men can be inferred from the Kouros statues and from Euripides' tragedy the *Ion*.[12] It is always 'life in myth' *for a definite period.* This above all was the purpose served by the festivals, and it is these which, side by side with mythology, we must now consider.

OLYMPIA

and the cults of Zeus and Hera

5 *A view from the ancient site of Olympia into the surrounding landscape*

6 *The archway leading from the stadium to the temples of Olympia*

7 *The ruins of the Temple of Zeus, Olympia*

8 *The remains of the western end of the Temple of Hera at Olympia*

9 *The Temple of Hera at Olympia, seen from the east*

10 *Zeus abducting
Ganymede:
terracotta statue by a
Peloponnesian artist,
c. 470 B.C.
Olympia Museum*

12 *A faience statuette of
Hera standing. Tegea,
early 4th century B.C.
British Museum*

11 *Fragment of a statuette
of Hera seated. Paestum,
early 4th century B.C.
British Museum*

13 *Two girls in a ritual dance. Metope from the Temple of Hera at the mouth of the River Sele, Paestum, Italian–Greek sculptor, late 6th century B.C. Paestum Museum*

14 *Hera unveils herself to Zeus. Metope from the east side of the Temple of Hera at Selinus, c. 460 B.C. National Museum, Palermo*

15 *Head of Hera; a detail from the metope in Plate 14*

16 *Head of Zeus; a detail from the metope in Plate 14*

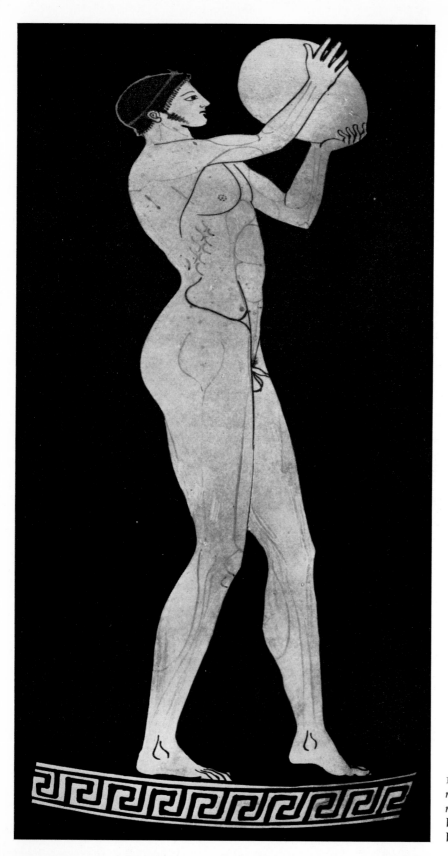

17 *Discus thrower
represented on a
red-figured vase found at
Vulci. 5th century B.C.
Vatican Museum*

18 *Vase painting showing Hera enthroned; from Tomb 127 in the Valle Trebba, Spina. Archaeological Museum, Ferrara*

19 *The wedding of Hera and Zeus. Attic black-figured vase from Kameiros. British Museum*

20 *These marble statues of Zeus and Pelops are two of the three centre figures from the east pediment of the Temple of Zeus at Olympia. Before 456 B.C. Olympia Museum*

21 *The two Dioscuri, sons of the Gods: Pollux on horseback, Castor on foot. By the Penthesilea painter, c. 460–450 B.C. Tomb 18c in the Valle Pega, Spina. Archaeological Museum, Ferrara*

CHAPTER II

The Feast

I

ANCIENT MAN, THE GREEK AND THE ROMAN, when he entered the presence of godhead, was confronted by a world of gods. And this world which showed him its mythological aspect in the gods was not another world, but that in which he lived.[13] The figures which peopled his world of gods were not less real to him because they originated from men and had no basis outside the world of men. The assurance that certain definite figures would reappear at definite times was continually sustained by the perception of cosmic recurrences. Ancient religion rests not so much on the belief that the tales told by mythology in all their contradictory variations are true (the question of truth never arises), but first and foremost on the certainty that the cosmos, an ordered universe, exists—a coherent and continuous foundation and background for whatever it is which shows its human face in mythology.

The word *cosmos* is to be understood here in its original Greek meaning, as the reality of the world in a definite state, involving the validity of a definite spiritual order.[14] This order is one possible mode of being of the world content, and it can just as well express itself in a mythological way, through divine figures, as in the various artistic or scientific ways, through artistic or scientific ideas. The term 'idea' must here be understood in a sense wide enough to include the divine figures themselves as *mythological ideas*. The correspondence between an *archetypal* world of gods and an *ectypal* world of men, which is to be found in any living mythology, was best expressed in the language of the Platonists in the previous chapter. The spiritual order which for the Greeks showed itself in Nature, as a world order, may be called the ideal aspect of the world, but the highest manifestation of this aspect in the feast may be called divine.

The world was not everywhere comprehended in this Greek fashion, through divine figures which even in their contradictoriness have the effect

C

of pure ideas. But all world orders—even those of the ancient East, the ancient American, and the rest—are intellectual in so far as one possible mode of the world's existence is realised in them through the knowing and ordering activity of the intellect, so that instead of the world itself we have a world picture. The different forms of this activity are spoken of as different forms of thought. The structure of any such form of thought and the world picture corresponding to it can be described in the same terms as the structure of a language.

A religion, however, is never based only on an empty order, an order without content, but at the same time on what is ordered: never only on a world picture, but always on the world reality—that is, on that which the reality of the world is for man. Whenever the world picture changes with time, it is always believed that the 'real world' has thereby been brought nearer. This belief is the source of those shocks to immediate certainty which cause the decline of religions. The reality of a religious idea—especially that of a divine figure—never depends on the form of thought but on the fact that this form—or in the case of divine figures this vision—is felt as valid. In other words, it depends on the assurance that it is the true reality of the world which is being viewed and declared in this way. We shall be turning our attention to one source of this certainty when we now concern ourselves with the nature of the religious festival.

2

'To know one religion is to know none'—such is the axiom which might serve as an introductory motto to every work on religion.[15] We can link it with another, expounded in the first chapter, which can be stated as: 'Living substance can be understood only in the live state'. Ancient religion —'the Religion of the Greeks and Romans'—is spiritually so close to us westerners as an historical phenomenon that we can immediately grasp its structure. It is a religion which is not directed towards the other world. Its gods are the gods of this world and of human Existence. Such divinities are transcendent only in so far as our Existence does not comprehend them, but they comprehend it. They are more than gods of life, they are also the gods of death and of that which surrounds us. And yet again this religion is so far away from us in time, its figures, where they are accessible to us at all, show themselves so complete and perfect, that it is impossible for us also to grasp it *in flagrante*, as a live thing, a perpetually self-renewing, living phenomenon. The explorer of ancient religion must look around him. What is there to be observed in other religions which can contribute to the understanding of the Greek and Roman religion?

The religion of peoples which have remained in a savage state appears to us by contrast quite alien, the most alien thing, indeed, which we can imagine. But wherever such a religion was still to be found, the anthropologists encountered it literally still alive, as a perpetually self-renewing, living entity. Such self-renewal is seldom more than a pure repetition. Primitive peoples know this. They repeat, consciously and exactly, the religious acts of their ancestors. This constitutes one principle of their religion. By repetition life loses strength, the living loses life itself. And yet at every repetition of a religious act some element of the creative is left over, something which can never be recovered once the act has ceased to be repeated. What we expect from anthropological research into religion is to be brought in closer contact with this live creative element.

It is only made clear what this element is when we turn from the life of a religion to its intellectual content. The intellectual aspect is more accessible to scientific study and easier to grasp than the living substance. In reality, of course, they do not exclude one another. If we wanted to start by making a separation between the two, between the vital and the meaningful, we should have to give special reasons for doing so. Neither the classical nor the anthropological material offers such a separation as a matter of course. On the contrary.

The most primitive religion has an intellectual content, it contains an idea. Whether we explain a religion as a matter of faith or as the immediate certainty of the religious person, we must in any event presuppose a state of affairs in which faith was not yet faith but arresting evidence, in which religious usage was perpetuated and through which it expressed itself, perhaps without words but with the exclusive force of an emotional act. Both the historian and the anthropologist must recognise that a state like this, a state of coming into being, will always be beyond their grasp. Ideas, however, are timeless. And wherever they occur, wherever they are conjured up, they bring with them an immediacy and power of conviction which tranforms the ordinary passage of time into a creative moment.

All that we can grasp is the idea, the intellectual content. The anthropologist does come across such times of transformation—'high times'—when they still have about them something of the warmth, freshness, and originality of the creative moment. They are warmed through by life, penetrated by the force of ideas, and we shall see that the creative element, too, is not lacking to them. Such times are called feasts or festivals. If there is one point from which the understanding of ancient religion can begin and in which the religious studies of classical scholarship and the science of anthropology can assist one another, it is here, in the exploration of the nature of the feast.

This question does not concern ancient religion alone. If we wanted to classify religions according to the extent of their addiction to the festival—which would be a perfectly feasible principle—the classical religion would have to be reckoned among those which are most markedly festival religions. Roman Catholicism belongs more or less to this group, while Protestantism must be regarded as tending to the opposite pole. Yet the thing, whatever it is, which makes a feast festal remains in all its gradations a religious phenomenon of such outstanding importance that we must approach it with the closest and most sensitive attention.

We shall not do so from the temporal side. We used to be told about a peculiar mythico-religious 'sense of phase',[16] which for primitive peoples 'applies to all the occurrences of life, particularly to the most important transitions from one age or status to another. Even at the lowest levels these transitions, the most important changes in the life of the species as of the individual, are in some way distinguished by the cult, are somehow lifted out of the uniform course of events.' Just as with biological time, the writer continued, so it is with the demarcations of cosmic time. They too are accompanied by a sense of phase. But in both cases, in the small world of men as well as in the greater universe, some matter of fact, something happening to the environment, is 'sensed', narrowly observed even and held fast. A phase is that which *phainetai*, 'shows itself'. A sense of phase is a feeling for reality rooted in the universe itself. At this point the concept of the 'holy' was introduced[17] and it was found that a point of time or a segment of time, even time itself, could be just as 'holy' as a place or as the whole of space. The weakness of this phraseology was that it obliterated and failed to give due attention to that special activity by which points and segments of time are singled out and converted into a 'work' of religion. Yet it is that which must be the primary concern of the study of religions.

For the sake of brevity, we call it 'the festive sense'. As an experience it is just as real for the man who has it as his feeling of certainty about the existence of the world. The festive quality which distinguishes certain demarcations of time attaches to all things within the compass of the feast and for those caught up within this compass and breathing this atmosphere —the festive persons themselves—is a wholly valid spiritual reality. Among spiritual realities this festive quality is a thing on its own, never to be confused with anything else. It can be confidently distinguished from all other feelings and is itself an absolute distinguishing mark.

Just this attribute, of giving absolute distinction, may serve for the present as a minimal definition of the festive quality. It was once usual in comparative religion and anthropology, to say nothing of classical studies, simply to pass over this quality, as if it did not exist. As an example we may take the case which was once thought to be the starting point for the anthropological interpretation of the whole of Greek religion. Only by neglecting the festive quality was it possible for Jane Harrison,[18] with her biological inspiration, to sustain her thesis that the rites of ancient religion were originally designed to promote life. In so doing she failed to notice that the later religious practices which she called in evidence had none of the marks of being original. By contrast with the great festal performances of archaic and classical times it is more natural to regard them as the outcome of a process of impoverishment and simplification. This simple instance can serve to show, however, that the festive quality is always to be presupposed as a distinguishing fact even in cases where, just because it is a fact and taken for granted, it receives no special mention. The festive quality is necessarily present in every festal proceeding, even when only in dead form as an intentional show. And for that reason every explanation which does not presuppose it is necessarily mistaken.

3

Plutarch in his Table Talk [19] tells us of a festal act which was performed in Chaironeia in the first century A.D. It was carried out once a year by each father of a household in his own house, and by the *archon* for the community as a whole. Plutarch used for this rite the same word *thusia* which belonged to the great festival sacrifices although in this case the whole performance consisted merely in the driving out of a slave with blows. The shrub from which the switches were cut, the 'chaste-tree' (*Vitex agnus-castus*), is known to us elsewhere from myths and the rites corresponding to them. It is used for fettering and for the garlanding which in the case of Prometheus and for men ever since has been a substitute for fettering. There is no mention here of a mythical precedent, what is happening is the *boulimou exelasis*, the expulsion of ravening hunger—or to translate the first word literally, 'of ox-hunger'. To understand how this is to be interpreted we shall after all need a mythological tale. The accompanying words of the rite were, 'Out with ravening hunger, in with riches and health'.

Plutarch himself refers to another much more imposing rite addressed to 'ravening hunger', by the people of Smyrna, who burnt a whole ox—the usual sacrifice to underworld deities. In Smyrna the great hunger was called *boubrostis*, 'ox-devouring', and it may be that Plutarch did not recognise that it was synonymous with *boulimos*—a word that he did not understand either—but it evidently refers to a hunger so great as to compel a man to devour an ox. Both words presuppose a story. According to the authority quoted by Plutarch, Metrodorus of Chios, the Smyrniot sacrifice was made to the *boubrostis* itself, as if it were a divine being. But in any sacrifice to underworld beings the intended deity might be kept secret and a pseudonym be used for it. This was very probably the case here. One story of the *boubrostis* is to be found in the Hymn to Demeter of Callimachus[66]. The goddess visited it upon Erysichthon, as a punishment for having felled trees in her sacred grove. It was also the negative guise of Demeter, who bore Pluto, or 'wealth', to Iasion. It is very possible that the Chaironeia custom in Plutarch's time was nothing but a poor relic of an older, more detailed sacrificial procedure, to which there also corresponded a story from the myths of Demeter.

But even the minimal performance described by Plutarch had enough festive quality attaching to it to suffice for a minimal definition of that phrase. The act was performed at a level of human existence absolutely different from the ordinary level to which Plutarch and his friends returned after the performance, when they had a discussion about the name and nature of the ailment *boulimia*. They were the same men as those who had just gone through the traditional performance—the *nenomismenon*—yet outside the festal sphere they could not possibly have done as they did. Not because their action had no sense! The sense here is evident and no faith is necessary to perform a traditional rite. Whether a man has faith or not, he cannot carry out such an action except in a festive spirit, on a level different from the everyday level of human existence. Tradition it was that here replaced the peculiar inner compulsion to step out on to that level. If it had been intended also to replace the festive quality, the whole performance would have turned into something dead, grotesque even, like the movement of the dancers for someone who has suddenly gone deaf and no longer hears the music. And one who does not hear the music himself does not dance. Without a festive feeling there is no feast.

The festive is not identical with the joyful. That is shown immediately by the example just quoted. Here too the comparison with music is applicable. The festive feeling can be cheerful or gloomy just as one can sway in time to joyful or to sad music. But there is something there, in the deepest foundations of the festive, which has more affinity with cheerfulness than with gloom. Even in gloom itself, when it is festive, we find something which was perceived by Hoelderlin at its highest intensity in Greek tragedy and expressed in his epigram about the 'Antigone' of Sophocles:

Many attempted in vain with joy to express the most joyful,
Here I have found it at last, here, but in sadness it speaks.

And yet on the other hand at the back of all festivity, however joyful and gay, there is seriousness. It is the seriousness which raises the most ordinary joyful act, such as the wine-drawing and wine-drinking of the Athenians on one of the days sacred to Dionysus, to the festal level. It is, of course, not seriousness in the sense of being the opposite of playful. For the festive admits play, every festal act is in a sense a play, though again not playful in the real sense of the word, not play for play's sake.

This elusive something, which has affinities with the cheerful, the serious, and the playful, which is yet on good terms with what is most gloomy, boisterous, and severe, in a word the *festive*, is preserved for us by poetry and the graphic arts in those works in which the great festivals of the Greeks and Romans have been taken out of the past and enshrined in the timeless world of art. Classical examples are the Odes of Pindar and the *Carmen Saeculare* of Horace, the frieze of the Parthenon, the sacred scenes of vase painting, and those of the Greek and Roman reliefs. And yet on the other hand the high artistic quality of these works is itself a warning to us to be careful. Perhaps we may by reason of it be getting too far away from the living thing, which even at its highest points is not timeless but at most time transformed. We must first seize the festive quality not where it appears already raised to the timeless heights of art but where it has not yet left time behind and is so to speak emerging from it, where time itself with its content of experience is becoming seizable because distinguished by the festive quality.

4

This is certainly the point at which the anthropological study of religion must take the lead. But at first we shall experience a disappointment. The phenomenon of the festive seems to have been completely overlooked by the anthropologists. At most they have noted that ingredient in the festive which approaches the cheerful. One distinguished anthropologist, R. R. Marett, has written, in the language of Christian theology, about 'hope in primitive religion'.[21]

He regarded 'hope' as a 'primal impulse' of all religion and gave biological reasons for his view: 'The very thrust of the life-process, so far as it reveals itself, however subliminally, in and for human experience may be said to consist in a certain hopefulness—a forwardness of reach'. The festal rules of primitive religion are in fact very apt to follow the rising line of natural phenomena. Their grimmest mourning customs often testify to the irreducibility of life. This appears to a certain extent to justify the biological approach to religion.

Its insufficiency as an explanatory principle becomes evident, however, as soon as an attempt is made to explain a religious phenomenon—in our case a festival—exclusively from the point of view of a hungry or otherwise wish-impelled living creature. This is how Marett proceeds when treating of a festival of the Arunta—primitive inhabitants of the Central Asian Desert—and without even describing it exactly seeks to explain it by his own biological and psychological method.[22] It is an instructive example of a very primitive ceremony the festive character of which is immediately apparent.

The Arunta hold the ceremonies concerned with the propagation of their totem animals—as Marett himself emphasizes—not in the dry season, when they must be particularly full of wishes, but at the very time when they can find abundant food. I should add too that they do it at the season when the particular totem animal does in fact propagate itself.[23] That is when they dance their festive dances. And they do not simply say, as Marett has it, 'We have eaten much food'. Their procedure is much more complicated. The chieftain pushes the others in the stomach with a stone, known as 'churinga unchima' and specially connected with the totem animal to be propagated, and as he does it says, 'You have eaten much food!' Thus everyone is supposed to be satisfied.

According to Marett we have here to do with a 'food dance'. It is danced with a full stomach as if to exclaim 'May this happy state of things continue'. But this is a rather arbitrary distortion of the facts. The perfect indicative contained in the ceremonial formula just quoted and accompanying the blow in the stomach is supposed according to Marett to stand for the present optative. But the Arunta language will not allow such an interpretation. I say nothing of the fact that such ceremonies strike the observer today as worn-out survivals rather than as having any originality. If they are childish, they are also senile. The 'idea', which is not lacking here either, no doubt concerns the relationship of the tribe with the totem animal. Otherwise we have here a case of a fossilised archaism, such as we encounter on classical soil in the games of the big-bellied Phlyakes of Southern Italy.[24] These were cult dancers before they acquired their stage, and kindred figures can be seen on Peloponnesian vase-paintings of the archaic period.[25] Their dances serve at best for an explanation of the 'food dance'. They were called forth by the enthusiasm of the full stomach no less than by other fullnesses. Intoxication by eating runs like a thread through Italian folk celebrations from the Atellan games of the ancient period right up to the macaroni and risotto eating at the Carnivals of today.

There are two features which stand out unambiguously from the ceremony of the Arunta: the festive character of the whole proceeding and its close connection with the time of year marked by it. I have described the festive quality as a special level on which actions are possible which would otherwise never be performed, and compared it with the way in which music creates a possibility for otherwise ridiculous and senseless movements. This level, or this music, is present here too. The carefully performed ceremony consists of song and stylised movements which can in the broadest sense be described as 'dancing'. The dance in this generalised sense is as it were the fundamental material of all primitive ceremonies and therefore requires some brief consideration.

The dance with primitive peoples all over the world is something much more ordinary and at the same time much holier than with the civilised. Leo Frobenius quotes an old saying on the subject: 'At full moon all Africa dances'.[23] And the dance remains in essence festal. It often serves, even among primitive peoples, also for entertainment, but has not there sunk to the level of mere entertainment as with us. It can be regarded as something quite distinctive, as an immediate, though not absolutely inevitable, manifestation of the festive. No Australian aboriginal would be willing to perform an ordinary, unfestive, immediately practical act through dancing. On the level of the dance, however, he will bring himself to do things which he would never attempt on the level of practical action—as for instance when in the intoxication of a full stomach he takes part in the propagation of totem animals. In such a case the dance is not a *means* to obtain a wish-object but the *representation* of something, a rendering of that which is valid for the dancer as an objective event. Marett tells of a '*profane*' dance festival, a 'corroboree' of the Narrinyeri on the lower Murray River which he himself attended, and at which these Australian aboriginals represented by their dance a steamer on the river.

Let us now turn to the second noteworthy feature of the propagation festival. The ceremony takes place at the season when the totem animal in any case propagates itself. In so far as the wish plays a part, the reality of what is wished stands beside and over it, a natural reality and at the same time a myth of the religion in question, compelling participation in the ceremony. Cosmic reality and intellectual reality cannot here be separated. The compulsion which they together exert reveals itself as a possibility of what is otherwise unusual, or rather impossible, reveals itself as the abundant power and freedom of a higher existence, as a feast. The biological and psychological reason for such compulsion and such freedom does not have to be specially given once we have fathomed the structure of the given phenomenon. The feast here too is 'life in myth', the myth of a vital principle identified with the totem animal and the repletion flowing from it.

5

The compulsion and the freedom of the feast does not in the cases quoted come from a sense of immediate obligation. The force of tradition is there too and habit plays its part. The anthropologist K. T. Preuss has shown with many examples how the festivals of primitive peoples are accompanied by myths which tell the story of how they first originated and hallowed by a consciousness of very ancient tradition. The same examples show how this same consciousness, paradoxically enough, is associated with an emphasis on the originality of what is performed. I quote one such case from his work on the religious content of myths.[27]

'Among the festivals of the Cora Indians in the mountains of the Pacific coast of Mexico'—so Preuss quotes from his expedition records [28]—'is one in which the young corn-cob is fetched from the altar by the woman who plays the part of the earth-and-moon goddess, his mother, displayed to the gods of all directions, and after the song which accompanies all the acted scenes and dances the fate which awaits him is expounded to them. There follows a great dance of the goddess with the calabash bowl in which her son lies. Finally he is handed over to the goddess Kuxkoama, who is waiting for him at the window. "Now she kills the son of our mother . . . Our mother weeps for her son because she has killed him. She is sad. . . ." In the next song, however, it is related that Sautari has not died but has gone to heaven. "It is known already to our mother in heaven" (the earth-and-moon goddess). Now his mother speaks to him. "Have you really not died?" "I have not died. Thus I know (how to arrange it). I shall deceive them" (men). "They appear only once, my younger brethren (men). Do they not die really for ever? I on the other hand never die, I shall appear continually (on earth). . . ." '

The conclusion that Preuss drew agrees with that reached by Malinowski in the light of his own researches. 'The song proves that this annually repeated celebration is here put on as if it were being originated for the first time. The participating divinities, whose natural destiny is here shown partly in human guise, go unsuspecting to meet their fate and not until the end is the perpetually recurrent character of the events revealed to them. The Indians said also that not only the divine personages occurring in the festival but also all those who took part in it were gods, that is ancestors become gods. The song here does duty for the myth, for, as Preuss concludes, 'its aim is to authenticate the present and the continually recurring phenomena by means of a single event at the beginning of time'. Preuss further adds that this explanation is applicable to every scene in the numerous festivals of the Cora, since the performers always represent gods or deified ancestors. The performance, he says, is always to be regarded as an event occurring for the first time. The participation of the gods in the ceremonies is not only thought of as voluntary, but the ceremonies themselves are directly described as their 'play', that is as a play of the highest divinity, of 'our father' the sun god—a play which the Cora are afraid to spoil by their own mistakes and weaknesses. They say the ceremonies were taught them by the god of the morning star when they were vainly trying to begin them on their own.

This saying of the Cora clearly brings out what it is which makes such performances at all possible. It is the festive quality, the decisive ingredient which has been overlooked by Preuss just as completely as by the other anthropologists. He notices and emphasizes only what is given as an explanation of the festive to unfestive people. Everywhere and always it is said to be *nenomismenon*, sacred tradition, pleasing to the gods, their command and their directive. It must be remembered, of course, that after Malinowski, and no doubt independently of him, Preuss was the anthropologist who demonstrated the great part played by myths in the religion of an archaic people. He did this by showing, first, that mythical tales contain the ideas which are carried out in the cult, among them the idea of the divine inauguration of the cult itself, and secondly, that the telling of a mythological tale is often itself a cult procedure. Between the telling and the performance there is in fact only a difference of degree, not of essence. Both cult procedure and mythological tale correspond to the same realities, psychic and cosmic, which can just as well be performed directly as viewed in figures or comprehended in narratives.

It is not to be wondered at that Preuss, whose attention was concentrated on the traditional character of cult procedures, did not notice their immediacy. For him, as for almost all anthropologists, a cult procedure was a magical procedure designed to achieve an effect. The fact is, however, that for most religions it would be too subtle a distinction to say that the mythological happening *brought* about the imitation in the cult procedure, but did not *happen* in order to bring it about. It was only gradually that men in their cult imitations allowed the idea of purpose more and more to gain the upper hand. Such a procedure, moreover, so Preuss explains, 'in virtue of the myth, is sanctified by ancestral practice from the beginning of time, and so is by no means a mere human act of will but a heavy duty, on the execution of which, in a manner corresponding to its first performance, the weal and woe of the people depend'. This illuminating but one-sided account of the festivals of primitive religions, as given by Preuss, seems to be in complete contradiction to the phenomena we have been discussing, the freedom of the festive feeling and the immediacy of cult procedures. For Preuss these procedures grew out of a sense of duty and were done from it.

This contradiction disappears when we turn to the statement of the Cora that they tried in vain to begin their ceremonies until they were taught them by the god Hatsikan. A purely human effort, the doing of an ordinary duty, is not a festival, and from a non-festive beginning a festival can be neither held nor understood. Something divine must be added, to make possible what is otherwise impossible. We are raised to a level where everything is 'as on the first day', shining, new, and 'happening for the first time'; where we are in the company of gods, ourselves even become divine; where the breath of creation is blowing and we ourselves take part in creation. That is the nature of the feast. And it does not exclude repetition. On the contrary. As soon as we are *reminded* of it by natural signs, by tradition and habit, we are capable, again and again and on every occasion, of participating in an unhabitual state of being and doing. Time and man become festal. *Et renovabitur facies terrae.*

This 'being reminded' is not incidental. It shows us an aspect of the feast which enables us not only to recognise it from our own living experience, but to understand its real nature. This is its intellectual aspect, by which its other, its vital aspect is completed. Not even the most primitive cult procedures are without an intellectual aspect. At the festival already described the Arunta behave as if the actual increase of the totem animal at that season had given them the *idea*, irresistible but agreeing with their wishes *as well*, of taking part in that increase. The idea in this case is the objective reality, become psychic and somewhat distorted by its human clothing stained with fear and greed. Whether the idea with its compelling force has been prompted for the first time by some reality of the universe or only recalled by it makes no essential difference.

The idea shines out from and through the divine figures as each one is named and represented dramatically, and the maize festival of the Cora Indians gives a particularly clear view of its structure. At the back of the maize festival stands the cosmic reality of the maize 'destiny', or life cycle, no matter whether the idea of such a destiny is new or merely remembered. How is it then that this idea takes shape among a people which live in an actual symbiosis with maize, as the destiny of an actual divinity, and why does it arise particularly in the 'high times' of maize? Could there be a more idle question? Something present has given rise to something more present, one reality to a higher one. And nothing can make the idea *more* present than what is visually presented at the ceremony, because in myth the cosmic reality is modelled in human substance. The nearest thing to man is man himself. Spontaneous vision or spontaneous drama in human shape—for in any original thing spontaneity must be presumed—is nearer to man than an animal epiphany or the imitation of animals in dance. The higher reality is no less true and its distinguishing element, the divine, stands out all the more prominently against the human, when it is represented by a human model. 'They appear only once, my younger brethren. Do they not die really for ever? I on the other hand never die, I shall appear continually'—such is the song of the slain maize-god.

It is an idea of perfect clarity and convincing truth. Although it is revived again and again in the same form through the ripening of the maize, it is immediate and original, for it only arises for men out of this ripening. The ordinary aspect of the maize life cycle appears again and again new and divine because of it. For men it is an immeasurably sad idea, yet at the same time it shows them the glitter of eternal things. Its conscientious execution in word and deed is a serious duty imposed by the overpowering strength of the idea and the sacred tradition. Yet to yield to this compulsion is suddenly to find oneself in the free 'play' of the gods, to raise oneself to a level of knowledge and achievement such as human beings are always raised to by a powerful, convincing idea.

6

Just as the festive quality was easily recognised as one among the experiences of our *life*, so too it now becomes immediately conprehensible as an *intellectual* experience. Nor have we here to do with a phenomenon falling exclusively within the field of the psychology of religion. 'Science has this in common with art'—so Nietzsche writes of such experience[29]—'that the most everyday things appear to it as completely new and attractive, or as if by the power of an enchantment just born and now lived for the first time'. He continues: 'Life is worth living, says art . . . life is worth knowing, says science'. In this he merely makes inferences appropriate to art and science from an intellectual experience which lies at the root not only of these two but also of religion and magic—inferences drawn from a complex and yet very simple and primary psychic reality, what he calls a sort of enchantment. Seen from within it is the experience of an idea, seen from its atmospheric exterior it is the experience of the festal. Our next task is to examine this *atmospheric* exterior.

It has long been remarked that these four things, art and science, religion and magic, are related to one another partly as like to like, partly as opposites. Attempts have been made to arrange them as stem and branches of a single genealogy. For Frazer the stem was magic alone, from which religion and art then branched off, while magic continued as science. According to Preuss magic and religion before separation formed the stem, and all four separately the branches. What is here overlooked is that the original primitive stem which in four directions divides into four independent forms of appearance must have contained all four in its own original substance. The experience of the festal is a point from which we can all start. And since it is not only part of our living experience but also, in particular, an intellectual experience, we can say that we *understand* what happens here.

What we must now seek to understand is a paradox. How is it that the festive can be in harmony with all four of these forms of activity at the same time, with art and science, as well as with religion and magic, or rather that it appears as an atmosphere common to them all? To return to our previous formulation, the man who yields to the compulsion of the feast—a compulsion felt with all solemnity—thereby takes part in the 'free play' of the gods. Such play seems to harmonise only with art, but not with science or magic. It does show some connection with religion, at least with the religion of primitive and older peoples, and even with mediaeval Christianity. Let us consider the phenomenon of play on its own.[30]

Play is something which entails at the same time the greatest compulsion and the greatest freedom. It entails the greatest compulsion because the player is completely tied to one aspect of the world, to which he gives himself over as to a psychic reality. He lives enchanted in it, in a special world. Boys who play at soldiers live in the soldier's world, girls who play with dolls, in the mother's. For that reason they are free from every idea of purpose lying outside such a world. Play is free from purpose. And in this respect it can indeed be compared with science. For the scientist or scholar plays when he surrenders himself to a self-chosen aspect of the world and pays no heed to ideas of purpose which might limit the free range of his exploration. The freedom of play is even greater than this. It is what the freedom of science can never be, arbitrariness. The man at play shapes the whole world to a world of his own and becomes thereby its creator and god. Play is power, and in that it is like magic. Where it is distinct from magic is in its freedom from the idea of purpose. That is why the freedom of play is so ethereally free, regardless of its self-chosen constraint. That is why the playful existence is happier and less substantial than the festive.

The festive atmosphere alternates between the serious and the playful, between close constraint and absolute freedom. Here is the paradox, and it disappears when we consider the festive in its essential aspect, in the light of the idea. Some ingredient of the real world becomes for the celebrant a psychic reality, an idea, lighting up in him and carrying instant conviction. From something present it becomes something even more present. What is it, then, this more present thing? Let us for a moment disregard the human figures which mediate it and consider only the idea which shines out through them. What is it? Something alien, existing independently of us and acting upon us, or our own creation which continues to be acted upon, among other things, by ourselves? Here is the paradox of the idea as intellectual experience, the paradox of creation itself. Not simply that creation in its nature does not exclude reality. Not simply that any form of artistic creation which did not assert something thought of as real in our universe would be unthinkable. But rather that the artist only has in himself and awakens in others the consciousness of real *making* when there comes forth from his hands something real, existent on its own, and grasped with respectful devotion. The birth of a reality thus grasped, of an idea, is constrained like science and play, but powerful and arbitrary like magic; in short, festal. All that art does is to hold fast the festive quality of such a birth, to confer permanence on the festive moment and on that which is pictured there or streams out of it like music: to raise the festal time to a timeless feast.

Creation is a festive affair in contrast to daily everyday making. (It was when the study of Greek religion began to talk of the 'making of a god' that it removed itself furthest away from any primitive or ancient religion.) And the festival always preserves, so long as it is a real festival, something of the creative, preserves at least the natural paradox of creation just described. Without a serious surrender to that reality which in the feast is represented, by word and deed, *as in play* such representation would be neither creative nor festive. Reality *and* representation together make up creation, make up the feast. Once the solid reality moves into the background so that the idea of purpose alone becomes dominant, then instead of the festal proceeding we have a magical one. There are many transitions and gradations. The character of play can be extended and the festive time be filled with special festival plays alongside the 'play' of the ceremonies themselves. Such distinctions become necessary the moment we turn our attention to individual festivals.[31]

The festival is in its essence creative rather than magical; good and efficacious but not practical in spirit. Festivals often demand an enormous

D

expenditure of energy, and for specially big festivals it seems that strength was collected for several years in advance. And yet repose too belongs to the essence of the feast, repose in contrast to the unrest of everyday affairs: a repose which combines in itself vital intensity and contemplation, and continues to do so even when vital intensity breaks out in exuberance and wantonness. The Attic Comedy is a case in point. The officious diligence of workaday life seems flat and absurd in the light of this repose, and yet the very things which in workaday life were most workaday and ordinary appear at the festival in a wonderful new light as worthy of special celebration. Handworkers and wine-drinkers, women and citizens at a festival have an insight into what it is which makes up their workaday life, a glimpse of something lofty and eternal, known to them otherwise only as their daily tasks and their daily business. For it is independent of them and they are dependent on it. The festival reveals the meaning of workaday existence, the essence of the things by which men are surrounded and of the forces which operate in their life. The festival as a reality of the world of men—for so we may call it, fusing its subjective and objective ingredients —means that humanity is capable, in rhythmically recurring periods of time, of becoming contemplative and in this condition of directly meeting the higher realities on which its whole existence rests. This meeting can also be interpreted as meaning that the world becomes transparent to man's intelligence and reveals to him one of its meaningful aspects, or alternatively, that in his intelligence the world arranges itself under one such aspect. The distinction of subjective and objective in this experience is entirely without significance.[32]

With all this it was not my intention to lay down any absolute rule, still less to generalise or invert such a rule by saying, for instance, that such meetings are possible *only* in rhythmically recurring periods of time, or that they have always been occasions for recurring festivals. Nothing of the kind is here intended. All that I may, I think, assert is this: even though we today cannot experience the religion of the Greeks and Romans as it was in its original state of coming into existence, as I have put it '*in flagrante*', yet all its cult procedures and myth-telling are accompanied by a festive quality, which is generated by a system of powerful ideas. This quality is in itself a proof that the ancient religion rests on such ideas and a guarantee that it can be made as intelligible to us today as the festive quality itself.

7

The *festive* character of Greek religion, which in this respect also shaped Roman religion, is balanced by its character as a mythological religion. The two aspects belong together. To view it not as a mythological festival religion but instead as a mere cult religion is to make light of the historical inventory in a way which verges on falsification. Such a view is pseudo-historical and one reason why it could ever have held the field is to be found in the condition of what has been handed down to us about the Greek festivals. We find here a desert with a few marvellous ruins. By contrast with it the mythological tradition, defective though it is, seems like a luxuriant jungle. For us today, confronted by this unequal balance in the survival of historical material, the 'beginning of wisdom', the famous *sapientia prima*, negative though it may be at first, is not to let ourselves be influenced by it, either consciously or unconsciously.

From this negative beginning the present book proceeds, like the reality of which it treats and which is still accessible, to the positive evidences, the monuments, the works of the artists. These are inexhaustible and allow us to guess at more than they show. Universal ideas shine through here too, the idea, for instance, that the gods and goddesses are pleased by beauty in their worshippers, male and female, or by beautiful animals and objects. 'Beautiful!'—*kalos* and *kale*—is sometimes, though not often, written beside their portraits on Attic vases.[33] We may probably assume that this exclamation addressed to the numerous beloved creatures on the vases had its beginning in the atmosphere of the festivals and was originally intended for the deities present there in their statues. To make oneself beautiful for the feast and at the feast to be as beautiful as mortal men can be and so become like the gods—this is a fundamental part of the festive quality, and it is one which might have been made for art. It is an original relationship of the festive with the beautiful, which, however, was never so prominent with any other people and nowhere so dominated the cult as with the Greeks.

No complete calendar of the festivals in the numerous Greek States and their numberless small communities has been preserved to us. All the same, by merely surveying and attempting to understand linguistically the names of festivals and ceremonies which have by chance survived—there are some three hundred of them—we become aware of a considerable wealth

of ideas, in that sense of the word 'idea' which we have adopted in this
chapter. At any rate the critical investigator is forced to doubt very much
whether they can all be derived from such simple 'vital needs' as the want of
protection or aversion. It would on the other hand be pushing the critical
spirit too far if, in the case of festivals associated with the name of a particular
deity, the historians were not in the first place to give some credence to the
Greeks themselves, who brought their worship to the one they named—
to Hera in the *Heraia*, to Athena in the *Athenaia* or *Panathenaia*. It is only
when the content of the worship, its idea, points in a different direction
from that consciously taken that we must look for *another* myth beyond those
of the named deity. These latter myths are the ones we must consider
in the first place. It is not often, however, that they have been completely
handed down to us.

Alongside names of festivals like those mentioned, which are derived
from the names of the deity celebrated, we find others which put the
ceremony in the foreground. Such for instance is the Hera festival of the
Daidala, the 'festival of artistic puppets' which was held on Mount Kithairon
in Boeotia.[34] The art and ingenuity were by no means confined to the
manufacture of the wooden servants of the goddess queen—for that is
what the puppets were. The mythical prototype was the wedding procession of Hera. In accordance with a long tradition, care was taken to
ensure the correspondence of cult and myth, even more, to harmonise the
proceedings with the picture of heaven, the cosmic background. Indeed,
the original performance presupposed certain refinements of astronomical
knowledge. The most solemn form of the festival was the 'Great Daedala'
which was celebrated every sixty years, according to the cycle of the planet
of Zeus, the bridegroom. It seems that we here find an ancient oriental
form of celebration persisting in the Greek world. It makes the impression
of a lonely erratic rock, but only because we know so little about the Greek
festivals.

There is one other festival in which the strength of tradition and the
association of ritual celebration with spontaneity show their power. Its
ceremonies began every year on the Acropolis at Athens with the sacrifice
of a bull, continued in the Prytaneion inside the city with a trial, and finished
on the seashore. The festival was called the *Dipoleia*, or 'Festival of the City-
God Zeus' (*Zeus Polieus*), but the ceremonies had a special name, *Bouphonia*,

'Bull-Murder', although bulls, of course, were killed at numberless other festivals. Through this name and the performance of the rite the intellectual aspect of what was happening is put very emphatically in the foreground. Not just one idea but two ideas in conflict with one another found expression in the ceremony. According to one the bull sacrifice was holy, according to the other it was unholy—it was a murder. The offenders were put on trial. Everyone who had taken part in the killing of the bull put the blame on the next one, until it reached the axe by which the animal had been slaughtered, and even the axe was acquitted.[35] It was the knife that in the end was found guilty[36]—the knife with which the animal's carcase had been cut up for the sacrificial meal. And this knife was 'drowned' in the sea as the real 'doer' of the deed. We may look in vain among the myths of Zeus for a correspondence with this duality and this strange judgment. There *was*, however, a myth of the murder of a god and his cutting up with the knife.[37] It was the myth of the 'Bull-Son',[38] of Dionysus incarnate as a bull. Here again we have a rock standing up from the seas of the older Greek religion. This is proved by the detail that it was not the axe but the knife which was punished. Memories of the unholy-holy proceeding in which the god was the victim and represented by an animal are otherwise more generally preserved through myths [39] than through such rites. These belong to an older Dionysus religion, not yet in the Greek style.

Thus far we are brought by the tradition in the case of certain Greek festivals. But the name *Bouphonia*, just like *Daidala*, is a neuter plural, and this is the form of festival name in which the Greek language quite generally expresses something of the essence of the feast. Festival names in Greek are plural, as collective names for the events and actions of the festal time. They are plurals mostly of an adjective which comprehends in its meaning and links with a common source everything revealed, festally, at that time. Most frequently it links them with the godhead itself, but often enough too with cult procedures, with the place of the cult, with cult objects or cult utensils. At the festivals called *Dionysia* there were 'Dionysiac things' present, in general that is, and not as it might be a quantity of some particular Dionysiac thing. The stem of the word denotes its outcome, in which all its details are included. When the grammatical form of the word does not allow an absolutely precise indication of the source, such precision is probably superfluous, as for instance in the case of the *Lenaia*, a winter festival of

Dionysus in Attica. The word-stem may be *lenos*, the wine-press, *lenai*, the women of the wine-press, of the *Lenaion*, the holy wine-press house and courtyard of Dionysus in Athens, all contributors to the source from which, after the fermentation and first clarification of the wine, the festive state flowed forth. All this formed with the time of the festival—the cosmic background—a distinct atmosphere which was 'Lenaean', not to be confused with anything else, and it called forth from the Athenians the Comedy, which became a further 'Lenaean' element. Or to take another example, the Dionysiac period next in the Athenian calendar, the festival cycle of the *Athesteria*, a name which enshrined the blossom-giving, growth-promoting properties of the god, included the day of the *Pithoigia*, on which the *Pithoi*, the great jars which held the now mature wine, were opened. The occurrence of the female substantive *Pithoigia* to describe this whole day signifies an impoverishment of the original festive occasion, which only the atmospheric plural adjective could convey. It has become a 'fossilised' piece of observance, nothing more than the cult action.

The Greek usage has an exact counterpart in the names of Roman festivals, the adjectival plurals with the ending *-alia*, *-ilia*, such as the *Matron-alia* or *Parilia*. Ovid in his calendar poem, the *Fasti*, shows himself no mean interpreter in feeling out the atmospheric and mythical content of such names. It is true he brings together a great deal from the most different times and sources, yet the names really asked to be filled out in this way. So long as we know no more than we do about the Etruscan festival names, we cannot judge how much Greek modes of expression contributed to their formation as well. The culture of the sixth century B.C. was distinguished not only in Greece but also in Etruria by a special joy in festivals and probably also by a special art in shaping them. And this Etruscan festival art was probably just as closely related to the corresponding Greek art as was Etruscan art generally. In Rome we meet at one and the same time with late and early, the highly developed and the surviving primitive. We must attempt at least to distinguish the Roman from the Greek traits, and this can less easily be accomplished through such complex structures as the festivals than through the simplest forms of religious experience.

THE ACROPOLIS

and the cult of Athena

22 *The Acropolis, from the Hill of the Muses. The Propylaea is to the left, the Temple of Athena Nike is in the centre, and the Parthenon to the right*

23 *The Parthenon seen from the east*

24 *The Erechtheum: west façade showing the Ionic columns and the south side with its portico of six maidens turned towards the Parthenon*

25 *A youth leading horses; from the Parthenon frieze, west side. Completed 432 B.C.
British Museum*

26 *Detail of horses, and a youth; from the north frieze of the Parthenon.*
Acropolis Museum, Athens

27 The Parthenon.
Frieze on the western face
of the cella, showing the
Panathenaic Procession

28 *Festival organiser and girls, from the Panathenaic Procession. East frieze of the Parthenon.
Louvre, Paris*

29 *Water-bearers, from the north frieze of the Parthenon.*
Acropolis Museum, Athens

31 *Bronze statue of Athena; a recent find in a sewer at Piraeus, mid-4th century B.C. Piraeus Museum*

30 *Marble votive relief to Athena showing the goddess leaning on her spear. Acropolis, mid-5th century B.C. Acropolis Museum, Athens*

32 *Pallas Athena in armour; from the west pediment of the temple of Aphaia, on Aegina. About 590 B.C. Glyptothek, Munich*

33 *Head of Pallas Athena, in Parian marble, from the east pediment of the Temple of Aphaia, on Aegina. Glyptothek, Munich*

34 *Athena with Theseus, Herakles and the heroes of Marathon. Upper band; birth of Pandora.*
Behind her, in the centre, Prometheus. Vase by the Niobid painter, from Tomb 579
in the Valle Trebba, Spina. Archaeological Museum, Ferrara

35 *Athena and one of the heroes of Marathon.*
Detail from the opposite page

36 *Battle of heroes in the presence of Athena. Vase by the Berlin painter. From Vulci, c. 490 B.C.*
Museum Antiker Kleinkunst, Munich

37 *A warrior and Nike, sacrificing. Over the head of Nike is the inscription:* KAΛH, *'beautiful'. Detail from an amphora by the Peleus painter, from Tomb 422 in the Valle Trebba, Spina. c. 430–420 B.C. Archaeological Museum, Ferrara*

38 *Herakles brings Athena the Stymphalian birds. Metope from the Temple of Zeus at Olympia;*
finished in 456 B.C. The torso of Herakles is in the Museum, Olympia; Athena is in the Louvre, Paris

39 *A head of Athena, from the east pediment of the o*
Temple of Athena on the Acropolis, c. 520 B.C
Acropolis Museum, Athe

40 *Nike at a sacrifice, undoing a sandal, from the balustrade of the Temple of Athena Nike, Acropolis Museum, Athens*

CHAPTER III

Two Styles of Religious Experience

I

THERE IS NOTHING TO JUSTIFY US in presuming without further enquiry that the religious experience of the Greeks was identical with that of any other people, or even only with that of the Romans, or that it was without its own characteristic features. Anyone who devotes himself to the study of religions and takes the obvious course of proceeding from a single religion, the religion of his own childhood or his earliest environment, is at first astonished to find what a variety of things in the history of mankind have been 'religion'. If as research worker and scholar he confines himself to religious phenomena, it seems to him as if religion forms a complete world of its own. This view, moreover, gains support from the analogy of another historical phenomenon—art too forms a world of its own.

The variety of aspects under which these special 'worlds' offer themselves is evidence of a profusion of forms, not simply in art or religion, but more fundamentally in the world of men itself. There is the mode of religion and the mode of art and this formal profusion can show itself in either. When we go further and say that what manifests itself in art is the artistic faculty, we make a more far-reaching abstraction which demands the greatest caution. The artistic faculty of man does manifest itself in this fashion, and human existence—in contrast to animal existence—does have this special peculiarity that it is artistic existence. But not all men share equally in the inherent artistic possibilities of human existence. The artistic quality is irreducible, distinct from all others, and it makes possible not only art itself but also a science of art. Yet it is not something additional, but a quality already given in the nature of human existence.

The religious quality too is of this kind. There are human beings and there have been peoples who possessed the religious faculty in varying degrees. But it would be a meaningless statement if we were to go on

E

from there to say that it is the 'holy' which manifests itself in religion.[41] What does manifest itself there is the religious faculty of man. We may use the word 'holy' to describe an individual who possesses the religious faculty in a high degree. He is the 'holy one'—the 'saint'. But neither the Israelites nor the Christians have in this sense esteemed God holy. Nor would they allow that the holy is a quality which merely *attaches* to their God. In those cases where something materially existent like a place or an object is called holy, there is always a tendency—today as much as ever—to think of holiness as something special, almost material, which is there added to it. We are told, of course, everywhere of *occurrences*—these are the special theme of mythological tales—which have once sanctified the place or cult object. There is none the less a universal tendency to conceive in material terms what this sanctification has there produced. This leads to the 'holy' beings, even sometimes the God of a monotheistic religion, being then conceived of as beings to whom holiness attaches. This is a theme of the history of religions, but it does not mean that 'the holy', as a materialised abstraction, would be a suitable starting point for the scientific study of religions.

Religious aptitude and religious experience seem in the course of human history to have stood in the same relation to one another as their artistic counterparts. For just as artistic experience presupposes a minimum of artistic aptitude, so without a minimum of religious aptitude no religious experience can be expected. Aptitude and experience belong together, and in the religious case both derive from that inherent possibility of human life for which we have no special word except religiosity. On the other hand, in the history of mankind no aptitude has ever yet exercised itself except within the Style of a particular Existence, in the sense in which I use those words in this book. Our task is here limited to understanding the Greek and Roman religions as the two kinds of religious experience peculiar respectively to the Greeks and to the Romans, and corresponding to two different religious aptitudes.

Moreover, however highly we rate the importance of the festive quality in our estimation of the two ancient religions, we have had from the very beginning to take account of two circumstances: first, that different degrees are possible in the festive quality of religions, and secondly, that the influence of Greek religion made itself particularly felt in the formation of Roman religion, either directly or through the medium of the Etruscan. On the other hand the linguistic apparatus of Roman religion, unlike the names of its festivals, is so original and so primitive by contrast with the Greek in its use of elementary concepts that a comparative study must put the Roman religion in the foreground, even when it is still concerned with what is specifically Greek.

2

The Romans were themselves aware of the difference of their religious experience from that of all other nations and considered themselves of all peoples the one distinguished by a special religious aptitude. This *religious consciousness* does in fact distinguish them from the Greeks, who in other respects were quite capable of being the most conscious of all men about everything. Indeed, it is quite possible that it was their Greek teachers who first awakened in the Romans the consciousness of their special religiosity. Polybius described with admiration but in rather disdainful terms the piety of the Romans.[42]   Not so the great Greek philosopher from the Syrian city of Apameia, Poseidonius. He in his great historical work wrote an appreciation of this religiosity as of something peculiarly Roman.[43] If he was the awakener, the consciousness he awakened was of something already there. His pupil Cicero makes a distinction which could only be made by one who had both, that which was there already and the consciousness of it.

Cicero even distinguishes the Roman from the Italian by reason of this consciousness. '*Quam volumus licet*', so the famous passage runs, in the speech On the Diviners' Reply[44]—'*ipsi nos amemus, tamen nec numero Hispanos, nec robore Gallos, nec calliditate Poenos, nec artibus Graecos, nec denique hoc ipso huius gentis et terrae domestico nativoque sensu Italos ipsos et Latinos, sed pietate ac religione atque hac una sapientia, quod deorum numine omnia regi gubernarique perspeximus, omnis gentes nationesque superavimus.*' 'However good an opinion we may have of ourselves, yet we do not excel the Spaniards in number, the Gauls in strength, the Carthaginians in cunning, the Greeks in arts, nor the Italians and Latins in the inborn sense of home and soil. We do however excel all peoples in religiosity and in that unique wisdom that has brought us to the realisation that everything is subordinate to the rule and direction of the gods.'

E*

Such was the clarity and determination given to the Roman religious consciousness by its encounter with the clarifying and awakening power of the Greek intelligence. But that is the most which can be attributed to the effect of Greece. The strength of the Roman religious awareness, with its claim to a peculiar relationship with the divine, may perhaps be compared with the well-known claim of the Israelites to be God's chosen people but certainly not with the Greek religious experience. And yet, so soon as we try to draw a parallel with Jewish religiosity, we perceive that the religious consciousness of the Romans belongs to the Roman Style of religious experience, which is not identical with any other, in particular not with the Israelite. The Jehovah religion is an experience of unmistakable demands which the chosen must fulfil. Their being chosen and the fulfilment of these demands, 'the knowledge and the fear of Jehovah'—as religion is called in the Old Testament [45]—so exclusively form the content of the lives of the chosen that we can no more talk of their having a special aptitude for attuning themselves to the divine, as Cicero has it, than we can talk of an art of interpretation where everything has only one meaning.

Greek religious experience forms the opposite pole to the Israelite, opposite indeed only with reference to the specifically Greek features on the one hand and the specifically Israelite on the other. If we disregard these for the moment, then both the Greek and the Israelite experience, in contrast to the Roman, have this in common, that they do not oscillate between alternatives which allow now a clearer, now a more obscure apprehension of the divine, but derive directly from presuppositions which are uniformly clear. These are for the Israelites the commands of Jehovah. For the Greeks on the other hand, the world which was the foundation of their particular religious experience showed up with a clearness all the more impressive for the obscurity of the background from which it arose.

3

The Style of the Greek religion has one characteristic above all. There is no Greek word or phrase for religious experience as a *special experience* or for the attitude produced by it as a special attitude. The Latin word *religio* does betoken such an attitude. Originally this word too was not restricted in its meaning to what is included in the sphere of religion today. *Religio* once meant merely 'scrupulous carefulness'—so we may render the content of the word—without necessarily referring to 'religious' things.[46] It only gradually became charged with the content of a special experience, the very thing in fact for which in most European languages there is no other word but the Latin 'religious'. In Greek the substantive *eulabeia*, 'carefulness', and the corresponding verb and adjective, *eulaboumai* and *eulabes*, went through a similar transformation.[47] In our texts this change first begins in the time of Plato and Demosthenes.[48] It was then hastened forward by the very circumstance that the Greek needed a corresponding word for the Roman term '*religio*'. The change of meaning was finally completed by Christianity. Today *evlavia* is a modern Greek word for religion.

Eulabeia in its original meaning presupposes no special experience. It expresses a universal attitude, which it was a duty to observe towards the divine, but *no more so* than towards any other reality of human life. Only the *reality* of the divine is presupposed by *eulabeia*, not some special danger which could *only* be associated with the divine, not even the danger that it perhaps exists and must therefore be treated with respect 'just in case'. At any rate none of the well-known passages in which the word *eulabeia* occurs would justify the interpretation that it is not the divine towards which we are careful but that we are careful because we are afraid of the possibility that a god might exist. The reality of the divine is not doubted and this reality is not feared in any special way. *Eulabeia* as an attitude is determined by the universal rule of life that in every one of life's relationships, and so in relation to the divine as well, one must guard against positive and negative exaggeration, against the too-much and the too-little.

Not only the concept of *thrasos*, of foolhardiness, is opposed to *eulabeia*, but also the too great faith which results in *deisidaimonia*, of which we shall come to speak shortly, and 'cult excess',[49] an archaic phenomenon which struck the Greeks of post-classical times as a relapse into barbarism. The internal motivation for this attitude is not necessarily religious. And yet with Plutarch of all writers, who is our chief source for these distinctions,[50] it is difficult to say whether they correspond more to the profane, philosophically refined Greek feeling or to the *religio* of the Romans—

such is the agreement between the two at this point. We shall have to return to this agreement when we concern ourselves with *religio* in more detail.

The concept of *eulabeia*, which in its religious use belongs to a fairly late period, does not take us very far into the nature of Greek religious experience. It only takes us far enough to be able to determine that for the Greeks the divine was a self-evident fact of the given world, in respect of which one raised not the question of its existence—as it might be in the form of a calculation of probability, like Pascal's famous bet—but the question of behaviour *worthy of a human being*. Differences in this behaviour at different times—for instance between pre-classical and post-classical be-haviour—are noticeable. When M. P. Nilsson speaks of a particularly 'popu-lar' religiosity of the Greeks, this is without historical foundation. The simple Greek was just as much on his guard against the too-much and the too-little as the philosophically educated Greek. Anyone who was not so was an exceptional phenomenon. In face of the self-evidence of the divine in the Greek world the concept of faith is meaningless. Here too the parallel with the Israelite religion is instructive. The Israelite's bond of union with his God was so much a matter of course that 'there was no need in the Old Testament of any special commandment to believe in it'.[51] There was the promise of Jehovah and trust in Him—the Greeks, it is true, had no such promise. It is no wonder that faith, or *pistis*, first became a fundamental religious concept in Christianity. Within the meaning of Greek religion it could only refer to the belief in the reality of the world. And this is the case with the Pythagorean philosopher Philolaos.[52] When religion is still in its unreflective state such self-evident trust gets no special mention. One may perhaps emphasize the credibility of a divine pronouncement—an oracle—and these demand faith, but only in special cases.

Foolhardiness and too great unbelief[53] are at the other extreme. Associ-ated with them in Greek opinion are some further contraries of right behaviour towards the divine. One, an attitude determined by fear, is *deisidaimonia*, another, a manner of divine service marked by strict observance of the rites, apparently a too great concentration on the rites themselves, is *threskeia*. The history of this word would detain us, even more than that of *eulabeia*, in the later period of Greek religion. The earliest records refer, characteristically enough, to the Egyptian cult,[54] and *threskos* no less than

41 *A statue of
Demeter seated,
from the Sanctuary
of Demeter and
Kore at Cnidos.
c. 340–330 B.C.
British Museum*

42 *A clothed figure of Aphrodite seated. From a bowl by the Lyandros painter. From Cesa near Betolle, c. 460 B.C. Archaeological Museum, Florence*

43 *A nude figure of crouching Aphrodite, in Parian marble, from Rhodes (see pp. 117–118) c. 100 B.C.; replica of 3rd century B.C. sculpture. Rhodes Museum*

44 *Statue of a priestess of Demeter, from the Sanctuary of Cnidos. The statue shows how the priestess set out to make herself resemble the goddess in appearance (cf. pl. 41). British Museum*

deisidaimon means the 'superstitious man'. The root verb *threomai* means the loud shrieking of women, which occurred, it is true, in the Greek cult, but was characteristic of Oriental religions.

The Latin translation of the word *deisidaimonia* by *superstitio*, which corresponds to the Greek *ekstasis*,[55] expresses the discovery of a relatively late period, that supersition and 'ecstasy' have a connection with one another. We should have to speak here of religious excitability. That form of *deisidaimonia* which Theophrastus portrays in his 'Superstitious Man' (*Deisidaimon*),[56] is no doubt a timeless phenomenon, yet on the whole characteristic of the later periods of religions. We are not entitled without evidence to generalise it to a primitive state of Greek religion. One reason why we may not do so is because *deisidaimon*, immediately before Theophrastus' use of it, that is, denoted in the works of his master Aristotle an aspect of religiosity which was easily reconcilable with *eulabeia*. According to Aristotle [57] the tyrant should try to appear as *deisidaimon*, that is to show his dependence on the gods—without exaggeration, however. The word *deisidaimonia* means 'fear of the *daimon*', and according to the most ancient use of language *daimon* is nothing else but that aspect of the divine in which it appears to man as his destiny.

4

There is a much more important Hellenic concept which would at once bring us closer to the real nature of Greek religiosity if it did not itself first have to be explained through a correct understanding of Greek religion. The fundamental concept of archaic Greek Existence which thus needs to be explained is the *nomos*. *Nomos, nomizein* is at the root of the whole of Greek religion in historic times, both in its cult and in its views about the gods—so far, at least, as it is not rooted in another form of the 'law', the *themis*, which we shall also seek to define more closely in what follows. One thinks about and worships the gods in the light of the *nomos*—*nomizei autous*. This stands for 'believing in them' but has a much more concrete meaning too, since it also includes the performance of the cult procedures which again presuppose the myth. The cult procedures are *nomizomena*, *nenomismena, nomima.*   An exact translation is virtually impossible.   Nor could it be otherwise, since here we have something specifically Greek, something belonging to the Greek *Style*.   It means not only a continual regard for tradition in *spirit*, but something more: 'to keep' what is handed down 'in steady, conventional use'.[59]   Custom and usage by contrast with the *nomos* are more unconscious and mechanical, law and order are too rigid, too reminiscent of express commands such as were never an essential part of Greek religion.   To speak of the development of a sort of 'legalism' at a certain phase in the history of Greek religion is to assume what amounts to a change of Style.   But no such thing, to the extent required by such a formulation, ever in fact occurred.

We can take a decisive step towards the understanding of the original Greek *nomos*-concept by recognising that the philosophic term *nomos* as the opposite of *physis* —nature—resulted from a process of reinterpretation and revaluation by the sophists.[60]   The *nomos* of the archaic poets and the older philosophers, Hesiod, Solon, Pindar, Heraclitus, even the tragedians, can be paraphrased in the words of Jacob Burckhardt [61]: 'It is the higher purpose which rules over all individual being, all individual will and does not content itself as in the more modern world with protecting the individual and exhorting him to pay his taxes and do his military service but *aspires to be the soul of all.*'   I emphasise these last words because their metaphorical manner comes very close to the language of Heraclitus, and that was not far removed from the myth itself.   'All human *nomoi*' writes this archaic philosopher 'are nurtured by one, the divine *nomos*'.[62]   As a poet Pindar is still nearer to the myth, and with him the *nomos* appears as an *almighty king* over gods and men.   The famous verses about Herakles and Geryoneus[63] leave no room for doubt that the source of the law's almightiness was not an abstract idea of justice or legality.   If it was an idea at all, it was rather that of kingship.   The *nomos* is *basileus*—king—and its power is founded in that. Yet here too it cannot be an abstract *basileia* which is meant, not the mere idea of kingship as a source of power, but the *existing world sovereignty of Zeus*.   There was an event, too which preceded this sovereignty, whether we consider only Zeus's ascent of the throne after the dethronement of Cronos or the whole battle with the Titans as well.   For the Greeks themselves the validity of all the *nomoi* became intelligible and started from this myth of an event that gave laws to human existence.

Zeus was the *king* whose will and might determined the world order. In the *nomos* there shows itself side by side with justice, *dike*—if this reveals itself at all—also power, *kratos* and *bia*. This was already stated by Solon,[64] and it follows with certainty from the verses of Hesiod which attribute the *nomos* to the ruling power of Zeus.[65] Pindar himself sees in the effect produced by King Nomos in the case of Herakles and Geryoneus the kingly pleasure and whim of Zeus.[66] In this concept of Nomos, justice is understood only as far as the nature of Zeus permits it. In virtue of such textual passages the *nomos* of the archaic time can be defined as a form of appearance of the World-King Zeus. Through *nomos*, *nomizein* the divine is presupposed at least as a real, existent power. The best translation for *nomizein* is 'acknowledge'. The presuppositions of Greek religion are neither *eulabeia* nor *deisidaimonia*, neither *nomos* nor *nomizein*, but Zeus and the gods.[67] The presuppositions of the *nomoi* are above all the male deities, while the female for the most part form a chorus of defining prototypes around the great goddess Themis.

5

When the words for religious experience and attitudes are negative, we must logically expect to encounter an assured presumption of the divine. We have already found a negative element of this kind in the word *religio* and also in *eulabeia*, in its meaning of carefulness. These words represent not action but only reaction. Now if there were only one such 'reaction word' occurring in the speech of more archaic times and reserved for the religious sphere, we should be entitled to call the reaction itself a religious experience and infer from it a quality of the divine nature by which it was distinguished from everything else in the world. Such a quality would be specific in so far as it could be attributed only to the divine. And it would be universal in so far as it did not belong to the structure of some particular divine figure, but was itself everywhere and in every respect the reason and condition of divinity. In Greek religion we never do encounter such a quality, even through the negative words. What we encounter is mythology and the festal manifestation of aspects of the world.

The case is no different with the verb *hazesthai* which might seem of all words that most confined to the religious sphere.[68] Its meaning is related to that of *dedienai*—'to be afraid'—and *aideisthai*—'to be ashamed', and it is used as absolutely synonymous with this latter word and, what is immediately decisive, moreover, it is not at all confined to the religious sphere. At the most it corresponds to *religio* in its original, 'non-religious' sense. It does not necessarily presuppose anything sacred of which we might stand in some particular awe. The circle of people to whom the verb *hazesthai* refers in Homer can, without changing its sense, be drawn so wide as to include the whole household of Odysseus.[69] For its slaves the word means a respectful, but certainly not a 'religious' behaviour. If we are looking for the most primitive relationships, there are points of reference in the Iliad which we must not neglect. *Hazesthai* is what Zeus himself feels towards the sphere of Night. He would not want to do anything which might displease this great goddess.[70] And *hazesthai* in two important passages refers to a deity to whom the epithet *hagnos*—'pure'—belongs, that is to Apollo.[71] In agreement with this is the fact that in the Odyssey a priest of Apollo is an object of *hazesthai*,[72] while in the Iliad Agamemnon had to atone for having failed to behave in this way to a priest of Apollo—here [73] *aideisthai* is used as a variant for *hazesthai* occurring somewhat earlier in the same passage.

The fundamental meaning of any word which is important for the study of religion is never determined by possible etymologies or linguistic comparisons but by contexts and connections within the language itself. The verb *hazesthai* in Greek is connected with the adjective *hagnos*, epithet of the pure and purifying god Apollo,[74] who in this capacity is also called Phoebus. In Homer *hagnos* is an epithet of Artemis [75] and Persephone,[76] even of an Apollo festival,[77] in Hesiod also of the goddess Demeter.[78] It can well be said that 'it is used pre-eminently of the uncontaminated elements of nature'.[79] Yet the elements have in the world of men their deathly aspect as well. They form, like the gods, a boundary to human existence [80] at which it must become aware of its own cessation, of the difference between mortality and eternity.

The other adjective from this root, *hagios*,[81] refers more to the cult—'pure' temples, uncontaminated cult statues, mysterious cult procedures, and it is believed [82] not to be very old, having perhaps originated in Asia

Minor after the Ionian migration, in the shadow so to speak of the great oriental-style sanctuaries. The preference shown for the word by the translators of the Old Testament seems to support this. But there is nothing here which would entitle us to identify with any foreign concept that quite definite thing to which all these words refer and which in the shape of Apollo and Artemis appeared to the Greeks as a particular higher reality, the pure, the unapproachable, that which requires us to keep our distance. Nor should we be justified in using such words as *taboo* or *mana* to clarify a concept which in Greek is quite clear enough. For either these words are colourless, generalising technical terms which convey nothing of the peculiarity and uniqueness of this purity, nothing for example of the different shade of meaning between *hagnos* and *hagios* in the passages where they occur, or else they have a special content which was to be found in certain foreign cultures but not necessarily in that of the Greeks.

It is uncertain etymologically whether these words are connected with *agos*, 'crime against the divine'.[83] In it the 'crime' is considered from a particular point of view, as a defilement from which one has to be made pure again, for which one has to atone. There is a problem concerning the relationship between the sphere of purity associated with Apollo and Artemis and the sphere of impurity denoted by *agos*, the sphere of sinful shedding of blood. This problem is not solved by saying that the concept of the holy was not reached by way of the Greek tradition and was itself ambivalent, that the most holy can at one and the same time be felt and regarded as the most impure.[84] The problem here presents itself from the beginning as quite concrete. *Agos* connects with the underworld, the sphere of death. The question must be so formulated: Is it unthinkable in the light of what has been handed down from archaic times that there was a connection between Apollo and Artemis and this sphere of death? The figure of holy Persephone, who belongs to the kingdom of the dead and is closely related to Artemis, guarantees the possibility of such a connection and the character of Demeter as *hagne* confirms it. The myths both of Artemis and Apollo leave us in no doubt of the deathly traits in the characters of these deities.[85] If *this* is the connection that the word *agos* in Greek vocabulary reflects, then we here encounter with special force an aspect, or more exactly a particular feature, of the existent world, in which two apparently opposite domains, that of purity and that of death, are in contact.

Not only the figures of Apollo and Artemis but also those of the goddess Night point the way in this direction.

6

The ancient concepts of religious purity, expressions which come nearest to the word 'holy' as when we use it without reference to any special theory, in Latin *sacer* and *sanctus*, never presuppose the divine in general, but always a special sphere of the divine, coinciding with the domain of Death. By one's personal purity one makes a constant affirmation of that sphere, to which one would fall victim if one were to lose it. The *homo sacer*—the person who among the Romans was condemned to be so named and so to be [86]—had fallen victim to Death. While still alive he belonged to the *di inferi*, the gods of the underworld. He might be killed but not sacrificed.[87] To make sacrifice was in Latin *sacrificium*, a proceeding which made the victim *sacer*. Anyone who was *sacer* already belonged to the gods of the underworld and could not therefore be accepted by them as a present, a sacrifice. *Sacer* meant the closest possible relationship to them. Kinship with a more friendly aspect of the underworld was betokened by the quality *sanctus*. We read in Cicero that while *pietas* refers to the gods, *sanctitas* refers to the *Manes*—the ghosts of the departed—and *justitia* to our fellow human beings.[88]

A similar concept with the Greeks is *hosion* or *hosia*. In our texts the substantive *hosia* occurs earlier than the adjective *hosios*.[89] In the Odyssey an action is twice described negatively as '*not-hosia*'[90] and advised against on religious grounds. In the first passage a plan of murder is under discussion, in the second the murdered men are lying there already and it would be not '*hosia*' to call on the gods and give expression to feelings of joy in the presence of the corpses. In the Homeric Hymn to Apollo the *hosia* takes the very archaic form of the non-use by men of the horses in the sacred precinct of Poseidon Hippios at Onchestos. It is thus shown that they are in fact sacred animals.[91] It is *hosia* if Demeter accepts the mixed drink prepared according to her instructions,[92] and *hosia* too if the gods partake of the sacrificial meat.[93] The dead man who does not receive that which honours him and is his due remains *anosios*,[94] without *hosia*, which is here simply defined as obsequies of the dead.[95]   *Hosia* is then conceived of quite concretely as 'offering', an offering, moreover, which need not necessarily be sacrificial,[96] but this was a later development.

Negative versions, like the quite general one that it is not *hosia* to plan one another's deaths,[97] are to be found quite early in our texts.   But this does not mean that the concept of *hosion* gets its positive content uniquely and entirely from its contrary, the *anosion*.[98]   In the Greek world a great deal had to be constantly *happening*—the gods and the dead getting their due —so that the *hosia* might be fully satisfied.   For the Bacchants of Euripides [99] the *Hosia* floats, a great goddess on golden wings, over the earth and, like another Nemesis, sees that everything is done the neglect of which might arouse the vengeance of a divine power, sees also that the whole world of gods, both the Olympians and those of the underworld to which the dead belong, receives from men the worship due to it, in the form of holy actions and the observance of what has to be observed.

Such is the picture of the *hosia* in classical times.   But it is nearly always the underworld which is meant when the gods are thought to have been offended by a crime against the *hosia*.   In one of his dialogues, the *Euthyphron*, Plato treats of *hosiotes* (the state of *hosia*) in a sense equivalent to piety and religious purity in general.   Yet he too starts from a case of murder, that is from the domain most characteristic of the underworld deities.   The acts of *hosioun* and *aphosiousthai* are pre-eminently a precaution against the vengeful impulses emanating from that territory.   *Hosios* as an adjective is specially applied to the purifying god, Apollo, who after each of his death-strokes must purify himself as well.[100]   A special group of *hosioi* was made up of five men who were the assistants of the oracle priest at Delphi[101] and whose special character of being the pre-eminently *hosioi* among all men derived from the performance of an animal sacrifice, the *hosioter*.   In general, in order to be *hosios* it was sufficient to live the Hellenic life as it was lived according to the *nomizomena* of the different States.   The dark background to this course of life was affirmed, but only received special emphasis in the case of the five of Delphi, who were said to be the true offspring of Deucalion through his grandson or great-grandson Delphos[102] and were, so to speak, the exemplary core of humanity.

The comparison of *hosiotes* with the Roman concept of *sanctitas* is an obvious one and also instructive.   As we have seen already, *sanctitas* above

F

all meant a good relationship to the dead. When Aeneas calls on the ghost of his father with the words '*salve sancte parens*',[103] it is certain that Anchises first possessed this quality when he was still alive and when he was dead only because of that. The participial form *sanctus*, which would be more exactly translated by 'made holy' or 'purified' than by 'holy' or 'pure', presupposes a purification or 'sanctification', an act of entering upon the good relationship meant by Cicero.[104] This must have held good for the original use of the word. When it is said of living people in our texts it betokens purity of life, with some religious coloration, but predominantly in a moral sense—as is the case with *hosiotes* as well.[105]

The word *hosios* is used not only of the person who leads a 'pure life' but of anything else to which purity can be applied, for instance a place where something goes on which is still permitted by the unwritten laws of life but would be forbidden by the laws of a stricter religious need.[106] Every State building that was not specially dedicated as a 'holy place', a *hieron* or sanctuary, formed part of the *hosia*.[107] It is accordingly quite clear that the *hosion* occupies a middle position between the *hieron* and the wholly profane. A division of ancient life into two domains, the sacred on one side, the profane on the other, is absolutely impossible. The epithet *profanum* —that which has its place *before* the sanctuary, the *fanum*—is late and was formed by elimination. Whatever had not reached that degree of sanctification which had been attained for instance by the initiates to the mysteries was *profanum*. *Sanctum* corresponds to *hosion* without being *sacrum*: *proprie dicimus sancta*—so runs Ulpian's legal definition [108]—*quae neque sacra neque profana sunt, sed sanctione quadam confirmata . . . quod enim sanctione quadam subnixum est, id sanctum est, etsi deo nonsit consecratum.* ('What we properly call *sancta* are things neither sacred nor profane, but bound by some sanction . . . for anything which is based upon a sanction is *sanctum*, even though it is not consecrated to a god.')

But these parallels also show up the difference between Greek and Roman religiosity. For the Romans the relationship to the underworld is more emphasised, and this dark zone of the divine stands unmistakably in the foreground. The *sanctum* is further extended in the direction of the death zone by the *sacrum*. *Sacrum* means the condition of being given over entirely to the underworld, while *sacrosanctum* means that which is protected by the threat of such a condition. The meaning of the Greek *hieron*, in its relation to the *hosion*, must no doubt be sought originally in the same direction. The slaughtering of the sacrificial animals is called in Homer *hiera rhezein*, which exactly corresponds to *sacri-ficium*. In the Creto-Mycenean texts the priest is already called *hiereus* and the man who performs the sacrifice *hieroworgos*. It seems that the words *hierourgos, hierourgein, hierourgia*, always retained a very solemn, almost gloomy sound.[109] Yet in Homer there is a complete absence of gloom about the sacrifice, and a change has already come about in the aura and atmosphere of the word *hieron*. To connect both *sacrum* and *hieron* with the alien notion of taboo is to ignore what is characteristic. *Hieros*, the adjective for everything which belongs to the persons or presence of the gods,[110] in Homer already has that radiant colour—if occasionally with a gloomier tinge—which throughout the historic period was peculiar to the Olympic world of gods, while *sacer* remains always unambiguously gloomy.

Even the *sanctum* contains a decided reference to something dark and threatening owing to the fact that, linguistically, unlike the *hosion*, it also implies the *sanctio*,[111] a ritual proceeding. A characteristic of Greek religion is the *remoteness* of the underworld domain, and this remoteness, though it varies at different times—also keeps the idea of the 'sanction' more in the background. It is part of *hosiotes* that the underworld domain is known to be in the background and at the same time kept at a distance. It is the quality of *hosiotes*, preserved in all situations, which keeps the menace of the subterranean beings at a distance. The world is stretched out bright and clear before the *hosios* and he has regard to all its aspects, as everyone is required to have, when he does everything in his power to ensure that the *hosia* is constantly happening all the time.

7

The life of the *hosios* is a normal life, pleasing to the gods after the Hellenic style. The characteristic of it is not a negative behaviour, but rather a laissez-faire, a *carefree piety*. A way of life distinguished by a special regard for the divine is called by the Greeks *eusebeia*.[112] Its root is the Greek verb expressing the highest form of worship—*sebein, sebesthai*. Here if anywhere we might hope to find a way leading through the phenomenon of this worship—called by the substantive *sebas*—to a full understanding of the specifically Greek religious experience. The etymology of the word group *sebein, sebas, semnos* (the attribute of being worthy of *this kind* of worship) is insufficient for this purpose. The etymological root meaning is on the face of it fairly clear and certain.[113] *Sebein, sebesthai* originally means something like 'step back from something with awe'. The simplest translation of *sebas* is 'awe'. This is confirmed, too, by the meaning of another verb derived from the same stem, *sobeo*—'I drive away'. This etymology does not require us to call in aid the mana-taboo kind of interpretation. The origin of the awe is no more expressed in *sebas* or *sebesthai* than the thing driven away is expressed by *sobein*. (If birds were meant, we should have to translate it 'scare away'.) Talk of the force of magic and its dangers, of *mana* or *orenda*—to mention a grotesque fashion which at one time invaded the study of ancient religion and of classical scholarship—is not justified by a single word or turn of phrase of the older Greek literature. *Dynamis* or *energeia* are not used in this sense till very late, in works which were written in Greek but had long ceased to be thought hellenically.[114]

To arrive at a real understanding, therefore, we must start not from the bare etymology of the words but from the whole phenomenon, an account of the experience, that is, in which its cause too is given. Opportunities of this kind are to be found in the Homeric poems. In the Odyssey there occurs in four different contexts the sentence: 'Awe takes hold of me at the sight'.[115] In no case can there be the slightest question of a mysterious secret force. The *sebas* is everywhere occasioned by something becoming manifest and present in an actual form, something which by its visible appearance is able to excite such awe. Thus *sebas* was excited in Telemachus by the radiance of the royal palace of Sparta; by the pleasing presence of Telemachus himself in the old friend of his father and in Helen, who discovers the likeness of Odysseus in the form of his son; and finally in Odysseus by the divine beauty of Nausicaa as it appears before his eyes. Gods and men alike feel *sebas* at the view of an appearance such as the narcissus, the wonderful flower which the earth goddess cunningly caused to grow for the enticement of Persephone and to oblige the god of the underworld—'a *sebas* for all to behold, immortal gods and mortal men'.[116]

Sebas can be excited not only by the beauty of an appearance, but also by a picture of horror, when it is imagined as if before one's eyes. Thus Achilles must picture to himself the dreadful state of Patrocles' dead body— 'The awe must penetrate his soul. . . .' [117] When it is the horrifying condition of a slain man or a dishonoured corpse which is being imagined, the atrocity itself need not actually occur. The awe of it is in the soul.[118] Again, it is the present situation which ought to excite *sebas* in the Greeks —'Does it not strike awe into you?'[119] *Sebas* comes from what is present, to the imagination or to the view, from a bodily and spiritual manifestation.

For in true Greek fashion it comes really from both at once. In the visible radiance of the palace of Menelaus Telemachus' inner eye sees the radiance, never yet seen, of the palace of Zeus. In Nausicaa Odysseus beholds the beauty, never yet beheld, of Artemis. In Telemachus the presence of his absent father is recognised. In the flower the wondrous radiance [120] of a divine enticement is perceived. In the pictures of horror and dread there is a mental vision of dishonour, something which from the viewpoint of an invisible norm is seen as intolerable.

The character of this norm can be realised from the following argument. We derive it from a phenomenon which can serve for an understanding of what was specifically Greek in religious *behaviour* in the same way as the phenomenon *sebesthai-sebazesthai-sebas* led us to the specifically Greek in religious *experience*. I mean the phenomenon of *aidos* or as a verb, *aideisthai*. It is in accordance with the Greek Style that *sebas* as a religious reaction formed part of the experience of a *show* or vision, a bodily and spiritual viewing in which the viewer and worshipper played an active part only insofar as he was the subject and not the object of the show. *Sebas* could be called pre-eminently a religious reaction because there was another strand to its meaning besides that of shrinking-back, of awe—the sense of worship. That is why 'awe' is only a makeshift translation; it does not render the whole meaning. *Theôn sebas* for 'worship of the gods' is a natural mode of expression,[121] while *thauma* or *thambos*, words of wonder and astonishment which occur in Homer in phrases similar to those in which *sebas* occurs,[122] have no such connotation, and if used in this way give quite a different effect.[123] There is, however, a group of words in Greek which have both these senses, of shrinking-back and of worship, the *aidos-aideisthai* group we are now discussing, for which 'shame', 'to be ashamed' are similarly no more than makeshift translations. The sense of worship, for instance, becomes clear in one specially significant context, where Hesiod describes the older, pre-Olympic gods as *theôn genos aidoion*, the 'shame-provoking generation of gods'.[124]

Relevant to this context also is the complementary relationship of *aidos* and *themis*, of which we shall come to speak. Themis as a deity belongs to the older generation of gods. Hesiod's phrase is a refutation of some widespread views on *aidos*.[125] It was seen as containing the central ethical concept of Homeric society, without the question being asked what was specifically Greek about the phenomenon as it was represented to us. The translation 'feeling of honour', associated with these views, is no more adequate on its own than 'feeling of shame' and it is the latter which comes closer to the reality. For it is wholly in accordance with the Greek Style that *aidos* too, like *sebas*, is founded on the experience of a *show*. The man who feels shame, however, is even more passive than he who feels *sebas* and *worships* accordingly. When a man also worships the one before whom he feels shame—for this is an ingredient of the phenomenon—he himself becomes the object of a show, the one who is ashamed. He is here not the viewer but the viewed. To feel that one is making a show of oneself, a show which does not fit into some definite picture of the world, that is *aideisthai*.

It is this quite definite picture of the world for which the phrase 'invisible norm' which I used above is a temporary and inadequate expression. For this picture is both visible and invisible at the same time, norm and yet a show for the mind's and body's eye at one and the same time. There is here no conflict between visible and invisible, moral and natural, spiritual and physical. It is something else which, on this world view, has not been evened out—the total world picture itself. The real world has several aspects and offers various pictures of itself. The show of a disharmony within one of these pictures is *aidos* for the one who was the unfortunate maker of the show. The true quality of *aidos* is explained not by the particular moral code of a particular station in life but by a disharmony which can occur in every station and in every part of the world. As these parts come into conflict with one another, so *aidos* can be ranged against *aidos*. The Homeric poems are quite clear on this point.

When Hector is waiting for his last fight with Achilles, the two old people, Priam and Hecuba, try to call their son back into the protecting walls of the city. The mother bares and shows her breast and with tears

implores Hector: 'Hector, my son, *before this*'—she means her breast—'feel
aidos and take pity too on me, if ever I gave you the comforting breast.
Remember it, dear son, and defend us against the enemy by staying inside
the walls. . . .'[126] As Priam had previously sought to soften his son with the
picture of himself, the father, dead, his corpse torn and dishonoured by his
own hounds,[127] so Hecuba's gesture calls up another vision—that of Hector
in conflict with everything which a mother's breast is and stands for. That
must arouse *aidos* in him.

The situation is at the same time full of life and full of meaning. It
makes an example for the intellect out of the living reality. The showing
of the breast, the baring of the body of an old woman and a queen, of the
mother's breast, is here against royal dignity and noble conduct but it is life
itself, immediate and unvarnished. It is no doubt an example also of the
particular art of Homer, which has earned him among all epic poets a particular
esteem. It is quite superfluous to give any special explanation for Hecuba's
action. Her gesture is entirely natural. Yet with it through every code of
caste behaviour an aspect of the world breaks through, a domain of the
world which possesses its own order. The mother's breast is a fragment of
bodily reality, and this, its corporeal nature, is what makes it meaningful
—all the more so for exciting the bodily reactions of affection and shame.
It is a symbol, in the sense of Goethe, who calls that 'symbolic' which 'is an
entire agreement with nature' and 'immediately declares its meaning',[128]
and a symbol too after the fashion in which symbols are used by ancient
art—as abbreviations.[129] As a symbol the mother's breast indicates a
definite world order, the world order of motherhood, and so offers the
mind's eye also a convincing show, a vision. For this reason, a thing too can
excite *aidos*, as does her husband's marriage-bed in Penelope.[130] It is the visible
sign of an invisible order, it can, so to speak, be seen through. It is a symbol,
not as an element of a symbolism, but as a transparent part of the world.

8

Not everything has yet been said about the experience of *aidos*. That the
highest orders of human existence can have physical and mental attributes

inseparable from one another is an important and ill-recognised fact in the history of thought. We must spend some little time on it. One piece of evidence has already been noted. *Aidos* really does mean 'feeling of shame' in the purely physical sense, though it also means something more. The word in Homer also means the sexual organs—*aidos* or *aidoia*—the very things, that is, which by their display, except in one particularly powerful sphere of the world, could have a disturbing, even destructive effect. Yet even the sexual sense of shame has its spiritual side, which must be considered together with the great psychic reality of sex in its more physical paradoxes. So long as we are talking of *aidos*, even in the cases where it means 'feeling of honour' in the language of a noble caste or 'worship' in the religious sense, the body is always dancing attendance. And from the bodily life there proceeds a spiritual order which, alongside the order of the *nomoi* and mingled with it, dominates Greek existence. *Aidos* in its most natural form, as sexual sense of shame, does not yet betoken an order. The order which does belong to it and gives it bounds and direction is the *Order of Themis*.

Themis in its original meaning is not a proper name, but the word for a concept, the full scope of which will become clear as we discuss it. It is complementary both to *aidos* and to *nomos*. We have already given a general idea of what is meant by this. Its close relationship to *aidos* is supported by texts, some of which will be quoted here. Everything which in our idiom is law, morality, and custom was in Greece *nomos* or *themis*. Whether more or less religious is of no consequence, since nothing of this kind lay entirely outside the religious sphere. When the mother's bared breast recalled the whole motherly aspect of the world, an Order of motherhood with its own demands, these demands were demands of *themis*. The use of language in the Greek is here quite precise, and brings us close to mythology. For it could just as well be said that they were demands of 'Themis', a great goddess.

The particular Order corresponding to the sovereign realm of Themis, which was more clearly demarcated for the Greeks than it is for us, was not a merely theoretical or juristic order set down in written laws. It was less so even than was the Order of the *nomoi*, but it was none the less a powerful Order and in this case one can well say an Order 'full of power'. Its 'powerfulness' comes obviously from its physical basis. It is spiritual only insofar as emphasis is laid on the idea of 'order'. We have to become more and more familiar with this paradox. Even in that which is emphatically physical there can be something appearing to the mind as an idea or a divine form which makes moral demands. The example of Hecuba just quoted is evidence of this inherent paradox. It spoke through a naked bodily gesture, though in this case it was not one of those which concerned the *aidoia*, the 'shame-provoking things', in the narrowest sense.

This meaning of *aidoia* and *aidos* is immediate evidence of the fact that the phenomenon of shame, which was central to the Greek concept of *aidos*, was originally concerned with the attitude to nakedness, and at that not a simple, positive nakedness but the contradictory nakedness of the sexual organs, both attractive and repellent at the same time. However, a further narrowing of the sense of *aidos* in this direction is unthinkable in terms of Greek development. For in that man's world nakedness became less and less shame-provoking, just as *aidos* in the broader sense of 'respect and self-respect' became more and more dominant. Peoples who go naked do not feel shame of nakedness itself but of invisible norms. These norms, however, regulate sexual life and there is nothing here to invalidate the coexistence of two areas of meaning, the natural ambivalence of nakedness on the one hand and on the other the invisible Order thereby indicated, the Greek name of which was Themis.

The relation of the concept of Themis to nakedness is quite clear in Greek linguistic usage.[131] It was an unforgivable offence against *aidos* of which Tiresias, whom we know as a blind soothsayer, had made himself guilty according to the story told by Callimachus in his poem 'The Bath of Pallas'. He looked upon the naked Athena and, as the poem has it, 'saw what it is not *themis* to see'.[132] As a punishment Tiresias lost the sight of his eyes. To look upon the complete nakedness of a goddess was an offence against Themis not only in the case of the virgin goddess Pallas Athena. It was so in the case of the goddess of love as well. Anchises, the lover of Aphrodite, shared the fate of Tiresias. He too was punished with blindness. According to a story alluded to by Theocritus,[133] the bees which were witnesses of the love-making stung out his eyes. Another story, that Anchises became lame because he boasted of the love of Aphrodite and was therefore struck with lightning by Zeus, has a less archaic sound.

Of the two statues of the love-goddess which Praxiteles according to the tradition made to the order of the islanders of Cos, the latter chose the clothed one.[134]   The religious scruples they may have had were to be sought in the domain of Themis.   It is probable that the naked Praxiteles statue set up by the people of Cnidos was permitted them only because they had previously worshipped a naked, oriental Aphrodite.[135]   In an epigram attributed to a poet by the name of Plato Praxiteles is excused on the ground that he himself had not seen that which was not *themis*.[136]   The painted Aphrodite Anadyomene of Apelles showed only her breast, which is *themis*.[137]   The waves concealed the rest 'which it is not *themis* to see'.[138] And if this is relatively late evidence, it is confirmed and amplified by a relatively early testimony in the Iliad, about the making of love, 'which is the *themis* of mankind, both of men and of women'.[139]

The rule of Themis in this domain, as we may now call it the heart of her realm, is not by any means only negative.   As a goddess she rules it, as a concept she is herself the rule which must be observed by gods and men both there and over a wider zone of natural relationships.   Themis in Homer calls the gods into their meetings, as she does also with men when it is a question of wider *themistes*, or rules of life.[140]   She is the first to greet Hera, the angry wife of Zeus, and feels sympathy with her, being herself one of the first of the wives of Zeus.   *Hybris*, or arrogance, which the Homeric Hymn to Apollo calls the '*themis* of mortal men', is thus contrasted with a *divine themis*.[141]   *Hybris* stands in express opposition to *aidos*.[142]   It is the ungodly themis, from which the true Themis holds itself distinct as a divine norm and rule.   The divine Themis operates first in the narrower world of sex, determined by the strict legality of female life—rape is called in Greek *athemitomixia* (copulation in defiance of Themis).[143]   But thereafter too it operates in the world of all human and divine communities, as the presence of an Order, and the power of this Order is attested by a spontaneous mode of behaviour, Aidos by name, which is a primitive phenomenon of all humanity.

9

In Latin 'shame', or *pudor*, occurs with almost the same meaning as *religio*.[144] But a connection between the bodily and the spiritual at the highest level is also indicated by the Roman *pietas*, a phenomenon related to the Greek *aidos*.[145] *Pietas* is closely related to *religio* and is translated by the Greek writers sometimes as *eusebeia* and sometimes as *eulabeia*.[146] Cicero and Christian writers use the word synonymously with *religio*.[147] *Pietas* has often been discussed in the literature of Roman religion as a peculiarly Roman concept, but its peculiarity was not understood. Scholars contented themselves with noting that *pietas* betokened an attitude of mind which showed itself in the mutual relations of parents and children, and in which, so they emphasised, a sense of duty, or a zeal for duty, was uppermost.[148] It was also stressed that *pietas* was Vergil's word for *religio*.[149] In this way the particular characteristic of *pietas* was overlooked.

We can get an idea of how the Romans thought about this phenomenon from the legend of the temple which was erected in Rome to the goddess Pietas. On the site of this temple, so it was related, a mother had once been imprisoned and had been kept alive by the milk of her own daughter's breast.[150] The story may have been adapted from a Greek original,[151] though this is by no means certain. But it would have been pointless, had it not represented *pietas* in the ideal form in which it appeared to the Romans. The special thing which here stands out is something bodily and spiritual at the same time. *Pietas* here shows itself as a form of absolute reciprocity in nature, a completely closed circle of giving and receiving. In some variants of the story the mother's place is taken by the father.[152] But the example thus revered is always this same natural circle of reciprocity. While *aidos* presupposes that one can also stand outside it, *pietas* as a matter of course unites those who give nourishment with those who in uninterrupted thankfulness return it, unites the sources of life with its creatures from which its sources receive life. The *pii* and *piae* are completely enclosed in this circle.

By comparison with the specifically Roman phenomenon, the specifically Greek characteristics of the Hecuba scene now become clearer. In order to explain the gesture and speech of Hecuba in Roman terms we should have to say that the mother was appealing to the son's *pietas*. In Greek terms she appeals to his *aidos*. As the mother's breast is made visible, the invisible Order of one whole aspect of the world shines through, and its showing is intended to call to the son's mind another vision, the vision of a hostility to that Order of the world, which he is bound to feel intolerable.

Aidos is worship founded on a convincing *vision*, yet it does presuppose the possibility of a revolt against it, a revolt against the visible world no less than against the invisible Order, for godlessness, or disrespect for *themis*, is also a possibility in the world of men.

If none the less in Hector the *aidos* before the maternal world is not aroused, it is not because he revolts against this world Order.   There stands before him a still mightier vision which arouses in him another *aidos*.   To withdraw now would be a violation of a world whose Order has made him the first among the Trojans, the world, that is to say, of manhood and responsibility whose symbol the living hero himself is.   It is the vision of himself in an unheroic situation which holds him back.   '*I should be* shamed before the Trojan men and women'—so his words must be translated. What he actually, says however, reads more exactly '*I am* shamed before the Trojan men and women', and he has said the same thing earlier on, when he takes leave of his wife.[153]   The experience of a vision or show as passive as that presupposed by *aidos* requires also spectators, a viewing *from outside*, that is, of which the active agents and performers in this context are the people who view.

The persons or things before which *aidos* is felt appear as symbols.   They indicate Orders seen only by the mind's eye.   Not only the mother's breast and the marriage bed, but also the hero who so to speak is shamed before his own ideal image, and the Trojan men and women who physically represent that Order at the head of which the hero stands, they all are symbols.   A symbolically transparent world like this which corresponds to *aidos* is characteristic of the specifically Greek religiosity.   Only the older generation of gods was called by Hesiod 'the *aidos*-provoking race of gods' —evidently because those of them who had not been thrown down into Tartarus were even more closely connected with the realm of Themis than the Olympian deities who gathered around Zeus and his Nomos.   In addition to Themis there was another of the primeval deities, Night, before whom Zeus himself felt that kind of respect for which the Greek word is *hazesthai*. Hesiod mentions one more of these primeval deities, one who is closely connected with Aidos and co-operates with her.   This was Nemesis.   She will help us to understand the situation which we have come to know as the Aidos situation and which may be considered as the key situation of Greek religious experience.

The Trojan men and women represent for Hector not only the unviolated world Order which makes him a hero. There lurks in them, so to speak, concealed but watchful, revenge for the violation of that Order. For every Order which is violated gives place only to another—the Order of Revenge. The personification of this last inviolable Order is Nemesis. She appears in the utterance of men. 'Nemesis will come upon me from men', says Telemachus on one occasion.[154] But neither men nor gods here have any choice. Neither can help making out of the timeless reality of Nemesis, which can never be confounded with any other, a reality for the soul. They do so by fulfilling and uttering *nemesis*—*nemesan, nemesasthai, nemesizesthai*.[155] All these verbs are linguistically and logically later than the substantive.[156] But the question whether the linguistic and spiritual figure from which they all derive was a deity or a concept has no more significance than it had in the case of Themis. Hesiod says without internal contradiction all there is to be said about the goddess.[157] Nemesis is called a daughter of Night, the cause of much sorrow to men. But whenever her primeval form fails to take on reality in men's souls and cannot express itself, Nemesis, like Aidos, has already left the earth, she is no longer there. She none the less inhabits the form of a goddess, a timeless aspect of the universe through which its Orders revenge themselves, an aspect moreover rich in mythological possibilities.[158]

The 'man of Aidos'—let us so call the one who finds himself in the situation here described—imposes correct behaviour on the show of spiritual Orders, a vision of mythological Forms which shine through everywhere, and Nemesis imposes such behaviour on him. In one epic fragment fear is named actually as a source of Aidos.[159] Yet where in Homer they appear united with one another,[160] *dedienai*, 'to be afraid', always a special kind of fear, is an aspect of *aideisthai*, for it too is supported by Nemesis. The Nemesis hanging over the man of Aidos also comes from the world of spiritual Orders, even though human spectators are its agents. A man's own *aidos* encounters the *nemesis* which 'comes from men'. But just as these men are not themselves the real avengers, neither are they the real spectators in a world in which the man of Aidos is confronted by primeval forms or aspects of the world. Psychologically, Aidos presupposes merely spectators, no matter whether men or gods. If at the same time she is correlated with a symbolically transparent world, we are bound to ask what eye it is which looks upon the man of Aidos when he alone confronts this world. It is true that in Homer the sun is named as the one who sees and hears everything.[161] He too is a great deity, in Homer doubly present, both in his visible appearance as Helios and in his spiritual personification as Apollo.[162] There is, however, also mentioned by Homer, a more universal, comprehensive term for the seeing or viewing that is incessantly directed at mankind. This term is expressly correlated with *aidos*. It is the *theôn opis*, the eye of the gods. Thus it is called in the Iliad,[163] and in the Odyssey it is said of Hercules: 'Neither before the eye of the gods nor before the table did he feel shame. . . .'[164] The table here stands for, is the symbol of, hospitality. The eye of divine spectators rests on men. It is a pure looking-on, and though the lightning flash of Nemesis can dart out of it, it remains essentially nothing but viewing. *Opis* means no more and no less than that activity which is correlated in sense to the passivity of the viewed. And yet fundamentally it too is passive, for it is pure receiving.

Thus in the phenomenon of Aidos a key situation of Greek religious experience is formed by the union of corresponding active and passive elements, seer and vision, viewer and viewed, a watched and watchful world. And in this we find that 'to see' means also 'to see through', 'physical' means also 'mental', and 'nature' means also an artificial 'norm'. The Style of this experience is preserved in *unity*. The words of Goethe's Lynkeus are here insufficient to characterise what is specifically Greek. The Hellene is not only 'born to see, appointed to view', *he stands there to be viewed*. He mirrors a world which looks upon him with open, intelligent eyes—with the eyes of Zeus and Themis, of all gods and goddesses both old and new of which mythology relates.

THE CULTS OF DIONYSUS

45 *The Theatre of Dionysus, Athens: view of the auditorium in its present form. 3rd century A.D.*

46 *Tragic mask with beard, bronze, found recently in a sewer at Piraeus. Piraeus Museum*

47 *Satyr mask from Samos; late 6th century B.C. British Museum*

48 *The Theatre of Dionysus; altar from the sanctuary of the god, decorated with masks of Silenus*

49 *Statuette of a comic actor, seated; probably from Piraeus. Terracotta, mid-4th century B.C. British Museum*

50 *Comic actor standing, portraying a slave with a baby. Found in Attica. Terracotta, mid-4th century B.C. British Museum*

51 *Satyric actor, representing Pappoileı with Dionysus; from Melos. Terracotta, mid-4th century B.C. British Museum*

52 *Head of Dionysus. From Temple of Dionysus, at Tarentum. Terracotta, early 5th century B.C. British Museum*

53 *Dionysus reclining, from Temple of Dionysus, at Tarentum. Terracotta, early 5th century B.C. British Museum*

54 *Comic actor in role of you woman; probably found in Athens. Terracotta, mid-4th century B.C. British Museum*

55 *Dionysus Protome, from Boeotia. Terracotta. 390–350 B.C. British Museum*

56 *Head of the young Dionysus; a late Hellenistic carving, found near Rome. British Museum*

57 *Hermes with the little Dionysus on his arm. Statue by Praxiteles, 330–320 B.C., from the Heraion, Olympia. Olympia Museum*

59 *Silenus plays the double flute before Dionysus. Detail from a vase by the Brygos painter,*
c. 460 B.C., from Vulci. Museum Antiker Kleinkunst, Munich

Religious ceremony and orgiastic dance before Dionysus
Hades, and the Queen of Hades. A vase painting by
lygnotos. From Tomb 128 in the Valle Trebba,
ina. Archaeological Museum, Ferrara

61 *Dionysus with maenads and satyrs. Vase from Vulci by the Kleophrades painter, c. 500 B.C. Museum Antiker Kleinkunst, Munich*

Satyr and maenad, a vase painting by the Altamura inter from Tomb 231 in the Valle Trebba, Spina, 460 B.C. Archaeological Museum, Ferrara

62 *Procession of Dionysus. Detail of a vase by the Niobid painter, from Tomb 313 in the Valle Trebba, Spina. Mid-5th century B.C. Archaeological Museum, Ferrara*

63 *Orgiastic dance of the girls (detail from the vase in plate 58)*

64 *Dionysus feast with Lenae (priestesses of Dionysus) before the idol of the god, by the Dinos painter. Found in Nocera. Archaeological Museum, Naples*

65 *Dionysus with Phylax comedy, a vase painting by Astaeas of Paestum, found in Lipari.*
Lipari Museum

66 *Dionysus at sea, from Vulci, vase painting by Exekias, c. 530 B.C. Munich Museum*

CHAPTER IV

Peaks of Greek and Roman Religious Experience

I

THEORIA

IT IS NOT 'THEORY' AS UNDERSTOOD BY CURRENT USAGE to which we now turn our attention. Our consideration of *sebas* and *aidos* has confirmed us in our view that these two concepts together were about equivalent to the Latin *religio*.[165] Their religious significance is seen most unmistakably in those passages of the Homeric poems where they do not refer to appearing deities or to events at divine worship, in the cult. Examples of their purely religious use, where they do refer to such happenings, are to be found notably in the Homeric Hymn to Demeter.

The appearance of the goddess in her unveiled person has an effect on Queen Metaneira which is described in the following words: 'She was seized by *aidos* and *sebas* and pale fear.'[166] The poet describes the sacred acts which the goddess has introduced in Eleusis with the word *semnos*—which is an epithet also of the dread underworld goddesses, the Erinyes, on whom no man may look, and has a common root with *sebas*. He does not speak of these holy acts and gives as reason for his silence—according to the most probable reading—a *sebas* of the gods so great as actually to rob him of speech.[167] To this great awe there corresponded in Eleusis a spectacle, a vision. This vision is only referred to by the poet, never described, and in such references all the resources of language are used to express one thing: that it was really, and not merely in a metaphorical sense, a vision.[168]

This visual experience which in its concreteness surpassed any mental vision and which was offered to initiates by the mysteries of Eleusis gave them a special standing in the ancient religion, transcending the normal

G

festal atmosphere of the other cults.   For this festal atmosphere could indeed be described as normal in comparison with the great festival of Eleusis—called the 'Mysteries'—which laid claim to be quite out of the ordinary. The Eleusinian mysteries show the direction taken by Greek religiosity but do not belong in this general survey.[169]   The Hymn to Demeter, though still in epic style, marks the transition to Eleusis, while the Homeric epics themselves do not move out of that atmosphere in which the essence of Greek religiosity, in its normal classical form, manifests itself, and which the epics no doubt helped most powerfully to create.   This atmosphere is a distinct phenomenon of Greek Existence, a specifically Greek mode of appearance of the festive quality.   It is for us an immediate demonstration of the way in which with the Greeks vision and festivity were essentially connected with one another and *together* constituted the highest religious and spiritual revelation.

The appearance of the gods in the Iliad and Odyssey is not an element of the cult.   It is 'something that happens', in an atmosphere which is no less festive than that of the cult.   For poetry, insofar as it is true and genuine art and really has the creative quality, is itself festal.   The history of Greek poetic art shows what are at most variations and changes in the scope of that festal atmosphere with which ancient poetic writing is always surrounded, never the complete disappearance of the festive quality.   Often indeed it is no more than a fleeting attitude of festivity which the poet assumes on a social occasion.   That is not the case with Homer, who is festive through and through.   The age of the great Greek festival compositions—the creation and artistic performance of festival cycles in the archaic and classical period —includes poetry in its festival arrangements as a pre-eminently festive phenomenon.   Examples are the recitals of Homeric poems at the Panathenaic Festival, the dramatic performances at Dionysus festivals, and so on. In Hellenistic times this wide range was somewhat narrowed but the festive quality did not change.   Alexandrine poetry withdrew into smaller circles, which even so were often still circles about the ruler, and the practice of the poetic art itself became an intimate festival.

Already in the age portrayed by Homer, poetry was a festival and had all the festival's characteristic marks, as a special way of human life.   Achilles in the Iliad escapes with his worries into the atmosphere of poetry as though into another more festive world.   There he can occupy himself with the vision of transfigured forms and events, exalted to timeless heights, while the everyday battle rages around him.[170] A banquet anywhere in the world has festive quality but alone it is not yet a festival. In the Odyssey its natural festivity needs the art of the singers Phemios and Demodokos to give it the form of a real feast, accompanied with dance and song. The relationship of Homeric poetry to the world it portrays is to be understood in general as nothing more than that of a more festive world to a less festive.

The appearance of the gods in person befits a more festive world. It is the privilege and consequence of the festive atmosphere generated by poetry, and in characteristically Greek fashion signifies a complete 'transparency', a transparency through which eternal forms are seen. For Homer appearances of the gods are possible, yet he does not believe that such appearances are the same for everyone. What he asks for is perfect clarity. Thus Hera in the Iliad says,[171] 'Hard is it to see the gods in perfect clarity'. Or in the Odyssey, 'For not to everyone do the gods appear in perfect clarity'.[172] Diomedes for this purpose must have the mist withdrawn entirely from his eyes.[173] Achilles and Diomedes both recognise the gods. This is the privilege and consequence of a special half-divine form of being, the heroic form. But it is also the privilege and consequence of the poetic art. Where the victim of events can detect nothing more precise than the *daimon*, that face of the divine which manifests itself in human destiny, or a divine action in general, the poet in virtue of his special faculty and his familiarity with the religious tradition can name the particular divine figure which stands in the background. This could be laid down as a law of Homer's narrative art.[174]

For all that, everything brought about by the gods in Homer happens quite naturally.[175] A great deal of an earlier, less transparent mythology was excluded by Homer from his poetic writing. His special religiosity consists in this, that he draws on wholly transparent natural sources for his inventions but everywhere recognises the divine in what is natural. All his divine figures can be followed back to their ultimate source in the structure of the world. It is moreover a mark of his characteristically Greek religiosity that he always views the divine as a definite figure. The difference between the knowledge of which ordinary mortals are capable and that realised by the poet is the difference between a murky vision of everyday and the clear vision of a festival. The festal world of Homer rests on a special knowledge in the poet, a *knowing* which is a *state of being* exactly corresponding to the transparency of the world. The transparency of the world allows the divine figures of nature to shine through for the poet, as for festive man generally. The knowledge attained by festive man, which derives from the mythological tradition but also animates the myth from personal experience, is the vision of divine forms shining through. The first realisation of Greek religion with which we can make historical contact was the Homeric world of gods, and this world was also definitive in prescribing for future ages the objective content of Greek religion. This content was neither changed nor added to substantially by later ages. The corresponding realisation of Greek religiosity—considered as a subjective experience—can be paraphrased as a special kind of vision, the visionary knowledge attained by festive man.

We have characterised the Style of Greek religious experience by this, that it assumes as its key situation a reciprocal, active and passive, vision, a spectacle in which men are both viewers and viewed. We have emphasised that 'viewing' or 'looking' here means also 'looking through', that 'physical' means also 'mental'. We have now made the additional point that it is the poet in whose keeping is the 'visionary knowledge of festive man', and in so saying we may over-simplify but we certainly do not fabricate. On the contrary, we thereby grasp the structure of a phenomenon which the Greeks themselves described in *one* word. In its subjective aspect they called it 'knowing' (*eidenai*), in its objective aspect by a word of the same root, 'form' (*eidos*).[176] The root meaning is that of 'seeing', 'catching sight of', and what we have here is not just etymology, but an essential truth in the derivation of two words either of which on its own describes the same phenomenon. Although it means 'knowing' *eidenai* in its sound-form expresses a sense of seeing—it 'sounds it'.[177] *Eidos* similarly expresses knowing. Less direct evidence of the same phenomenon is to be found in the fact that though Homer uses another verb for 'know' he is fond of combining it with verbs of 'seeing',[178] or that for Socrates and Plato, when they define pure knowledge as *phronesis*, this knowledge always has for its object something seen—the idea as a standard form.[179] For the Greeks the most self-evident object both of seeing and of knowing is the form, an object so self-evident that it finds immediate expression in the language, in 'sound'. Verb and object *eidenai* and *eidos* form a circle which cannot be broken without a

destruction of *Style*, a unity each half of which defines the other. This circle
is not confined to a single word-group. Knowing for the Greeks, whatever
word they use for it, is based *primarily* on seeing and includes a 'viewing'.
The Greek phenomenon *eidenai* would have to be paraphrased in every
European language of today as 'seeing knowledge', simply because for the
Greeks seeing was included in knowing.

This peculiarity of the phenomenon of knowledge is no mere primitive
or elementary stage in the history of Greek thought, but something specifically Greek which was still valid at least for Aristotle. For it is not a
matter merely of phraseology. Linguistically the fact that the verb *eidenai*
is formed from the perfect stem must be understood as determining the
result of an act of looking or seeing. For this result *need* not be a vision, to
the exclusion of all other possibilities, but is so identified by the verb. The
close connection between seeing and knowing long continued to characterise
the history of Greek thought. The Greek logician and 'ontologist', a man
of 'knowledge' in the most intimate sense of the word, always remained a
man of 'vision'. Aristotle in the introductory words of his Metaphysics,
his theory of being, praises the joy of seeing and viewing (*to horan*), which
may be entirely lacking in practical utility, but offers a better basis for
knowledge than all other forms of perception.[180] The connection between
horan and *eidenai* never ceased to assert itself either in the consciousness of
Greek philosophers or in Greek linguistic usage.[181] Indeed, the joy in real,
sensual seeing is even more evident with Aristotle than with Plato. Undoubtedly the latter is no less a man of vision than his pupil or than Homer
himself.[182] But Plato and his teacher Socrates had more to say about the
transcendental viewing which has for object the transcendental form than
about the seeing of the senses.

The inseparable connection of knowing and seeing not only had the
consequence that the Greeks at once 'saw' as 'form' everything that they
'knew', but another consequence as well. The known was for them as
actual and consequently as certain, indeed as efficacious, as anything which
is immediately and clearly seen. For Plato a known and therefore also seen
world could actually excel in brilliance the world which was *merely* seen.
And this was probably the case also with Socrates, for whom this world
had ceased to offer much ground for true knowledge, having virtually
lost its Homeric transparency to divine forms and therewith its brilliance.

In place of the world touched by the radiance of the divine there remained for the philosophers of the post-classical period, of whom Socrates was the first, a world merely visible. A world which was known and radiant, the Homeric and early classical world, had turned into one which was merely *seen*. It may have been full of beauty, but it was also full of impermanence.

Greek 'knowing' means a viewing which, directed at the visible world, encounters something which is timeless and to that extent also eternal, forms which are invisible and can yet become objects of a vision. When these forms at the back of the visible world retire still further into that background, they draw after them that quality which in the eye of the beholder clings to whatever is perfectly clear and actual—we have called it 'radiance', by a sensual word which comes nearest to the divine in the domain of Greek religion. Without that festive radiance this world of ours, thus left behind, must necessarily pale in all its beauty—as if it were no longer known at all. But so long as this did not happen, this world *together with* its beauty and the radiance of its eternal forms was in the Greek fashion *known*. This being known did not necessarily involve also being seen, but it did involve, besides the radiance, what I will call efficacy. By this I mean not the practical effects of divine working but an all-pervading effective power. Through the peculiarly Greek phenomenon of knowledge here discussed this efficacy made itself just as strongly felt as the indescribable radiance which in Greek religion appears distributed over the world in eternal forms.

Anyone who has tried to conceive of Greek religion without this radiance—the radiance of divine forms which were known even when they did not make a bodily appearance—has had to find a special explanation for the efficacy of the gods and has had to look for it outside Greek Existence and its Style. It is a peculiarity of this Existence that in it the 'known' is also 'effective', and that the converse of this relationship is also true—whatever has an effect upon a living being is conceived as something objectively known there. It forms a world domain independent of any knower, which is quite simply known by any being upon whom it has an effect.[183] He does not act like one possessed of powers or spirits, he 'knows'. When Achilles in the Iliad is savage as a lion, he 'knows like a lion savage things'. The Cyclops in the Odyssey 'knew things against the law of nature' when he devoured men. Friends are 'knowing of friendly things towards one another'. This is far removed from any philosophy, but it does explain a peculiarity of Socratic thought. By reason of this Greek experience Socrates looked for the motives of moral decision not in the will but in knowledge. And Aristotle too remains within the Greek Style when he recognises the moral value of this sort of knowing and regards it as a special category of knowledge.[184] To know means, as a matter of course, to act accordingly. Such is the power of the known.

What we have here is not some kind of one-sided approach to the world, a form of 'intellectualism', for instance, but the fundamental phenomenon of Greek Existence, needing no further amplification. It is, to speak metaphorically, round and whole, as Being was for Parmenides. That which is acknowledged and understood, the seen-and-known, is an efficacious power. It can form the basis of genuine religious experiences and warm and living acts of will. That is why the Greeks themselves, when they think about it from a certain distance, define their piety as *episteme*, 'science'.[185] This definition of piety as the 'science' of divine worship, assumes the Socratic and Platonic valuation of *episteme*. Thus it does not imply any limitation of piety to an observance of empty forms but rather allowed the highest possible extension of its meaning, to that true knowledge which relates to the eternal and of which only the gods are really capable. A godless man 'knows what is godless', a pious man 'knows what is divine'—so it must be expressed in this Style—and must needs act accordingly, taking part in the divine. The one who possesses this knowledge in the highest degree is himself divine, is God, is Zeus. Not only Socrates and Plato lived in this religious experience, for so we must call it, since the fundamentally theological strain in Greek philosophy would make it hard to distinguish here between 'religion' and 'philosophy'[186]—but Aristotle too, as his *Metaphysics* testifies.[187] The argument which he there develops at such length corresponds to the Homeric use of the verb *eidenai*, of which examples have been given.

With their concept of a divine knowledge which really belongs only to one God, to the highest God indeed, the philosophers do not part company with Homer. They do not step outside the bounds of Greek Style as it is already established in Homer. In Greek the occurrence of knowledge that sees can be formulated as follows: it is God when such a thing occurs.[188]

A divine knowledge which may also become effective in human life or which the philosopher wants to be so belongs to the structure of the Greek phenomenon 'knowing' as a complement of human knowledge. For human knowledge is something passive, it means that we are subject to an 'efficacy', subordinate to the power of knowledge, and act accordingly. The world is known, so to speak independent of man, but dependent on that higher knowledge which at the same time exerts an efficacy, has power, and, as we must add, 'sees' the result. This phenomenon of higher knowledge, an extension of *eidenai*, is *noein*. It has apparently freed itself altogether from seeing.

And yet this verb too is connected by Homer with the eyes, as their activity, and used with the meaning 'to notice with the eyes'.[189] Hesiod mentions the eye of Zeus when he speaks of his seeing and *noein*.[190] Moreover *noein*, just as much as *eidenai*, perhaps even more so, can mean the disposition, the mentality, the direction in which one is driven by a higher power. This is proved by the mythological names ending in -*noos* or -*noe*, like Hipponoos or Hipponoe, 'being driven by a horse's nature'. The fundamental meaning of *noein* seems from the beginning to have contained more than just 'getting to know' in the sense of 'comprehending, learning by eye or ear, perceiving'. With this word in particular it is not etymology that is decisive, for nothing 'sounds' in it except that higher, more powerful thing which *nous* was for the Greeks.[191] By *noein* the object of perception is apprehended from that quarter which escapes the organs of sense, but which can yet be apprehended by the vehicle of *noein*, by the *nous*.[192] *Nous* directs itself towards the world in *noein* just as the eyes do in seeing. Yet the eyes merely take in sense-impressions, just as *eidenai* too is merely seeing-and-acting-accordingly. The *Nous* is *more* than the eye of gods and men, *noein* is more than 'seeing knowledge'.

This 'more' shows itself first of all in the fact that *nous*—although it seems to exist only in *noein* and to have no other hold anywhere else—has an extraordinary reality and consequently also divinity for the Greeks. It comes easier to them to ascribe *nous* and *noein* to a god than to a man, and easiest of all to the highest god. Besides this, *noein* is movable. The *nous* is able at will to reflect something which lies far away, to be where a far traveller once was and would like to be again.[193] It can transport itself like a god over all distances and obstacles. And finally, as we have already said, this divine knowledge, without real activity or a special act of will, exercises 'efficacy', has power, and 'sees' the result. Indeed *noein* in itself means an 'insight' which is *immediately* realised in action. The element of willing can here be left completely out of account.

There are plenty of examples in Homer. A continually recurring phrase is, 'the goddess thought otherwise' [194]—no need to add that she immediately translated her thought into action. That is a matter of course. In Book XVI of the Iliad Patroclus might perhaps still withdraw even after the killing of Sarpedon and so save himself. But—nothing comes of it. The reason is so given: 'The *Nous* of Zeus is more powerful than that of men'.[195] We too have an immediate understanding of this sentence, although in Christian terms we are accustomed to express ourselves differently and to say, 'God willed it otherwise'. Zeus did indeed will it, since Patroclus had killed his son. Thetis speaks expressly of the 'will of the gods,[196] not in a wise speech, however, but in a reproachful one. The word she uses indicates something arbitrary, which can also come from passion or wilfulness.[197] Men are specially fond of blaming the 'whim' of the gods.[198] In so doing they show their ignorance. In reality—and this is expressed without additions or explanations by the poet's language—what here hovers over men as the highest thing is not an absolute divine will but a mighty *nous*. The words used do not even go so far as to say that an 'effect' streams forth from this *nous*. It is more like a mirror which reflects the deeds of men together with their results. To name it is to name a higher and broader insight.

In place of *nous* mention may be made of a 'plan' or 'resolve' of Zeus.[199] Or the poet may also tell of decrees of Zeus—as for instance at the beginning of Book II of the Iliad—which punish some human presumption. What is here presupposed is his *Nous*. Nothing can escape this Nous, for it is 'closely wrought'—too opaque for anything to slip through.[200] No other god has power to avoid the *nous* of Zeus by guile, still less to make it without effect.[201] The *noein* of Zeus means a perfect intellectual reflection of that which exists and must happen as a consequence of what exists. Zeus, however, can still be restrained from *noein*. His *nous* can, like the eyes, be turned off by another powerful reality of the world, like sleep or love in Book XIV of the Iliad,[202] or an incomprehensible bedazzlement.[203] For Zeus is not only his *Nous*. He has another part to play in the world than merely *noein*, which is all that concerns us here.

In the Greek sense Existence is seeing and being-seen, or more exactly, knowing and being-known, or most exactly of all, being and being-known. It is *noein* which realises that passive faculty of being by which it can be known. Thus we can paraphrase with deliberately simplifying words and the fewest possible strokes of the pen what for the Greeks was a fact of their Existence and found immediate expression in their language. In such an Existence and such a language the philosopher can go further and say: 'For *noein* and being are one and the same thing'.[204] It is extremely difficult here to insert a word from another language in place of *noein*. Parmenides does not content himself with what Homer knew about the *noein* of Zeus, that it is 'opaque', so that it absorbs being like a mirror and is not identical with it, and that it can be turned off. It is open to question which of the two was wiser, the poet or the philosopher. The latter speaks of *noein* in a new way, but he is still speaking of the same thing as Homer, and still speaking of that form of knowledge which in the Homeric religion was peculiar to the highest god.

Such higher knowledge does not mean that we have moved away from that Vision—the 'eyes of the gods'—in which the man of *aidos* is placed by Homer. So far we have only laid bare that aspect of *noein* according to which, in a manner not capable of further analysis, it includes within its meaning also the fact that a decision has been taken and carried out. This could not be further explained but simply had to be accepted as an essential expression of the Greek way of thinking. But in the same way, too, *noein* also included what we have discussed as Vision. One could call it pure contemplation, if it were not connected, in the manner just described, with Being, as this is continually manifest in human affairs. Provided we do not forget this, we may speak of a contemplative Zeus in the Iliad. The Greek law of Style demands an onlooker, and Zeus as he is portrayed by Homer is tireless at looking on.

The Homeric Zeus, whose *Nous* rules the world, and who can therefore not be stamped as a deus *otiosus*, an 'idle god' such as the anthropologists have found among archaic peooles of today—Zeus is the spectator who completes the picture of the world as it appears to Greek religious experience. For the Greeks the standpoint of the spectator is in itself divine. To adopt this standpoint means for them the divine fulfilment of existence. Their philosophers aspire to it [205] and hope to be able to reach this fulfilment.

The reason for their hope lies embedded in the form of Greek religious experience, and it had two points of highest intensity, or 'peaks'. The first of these was seeing the gods face to face. When such a vision occurred, the Greek word *theos* would have to be uttered in its exact predicative sense, for which the Latin *ecce deus* would be an equivalent.[206] The second peak experience was to see like the gods. Anyone having such a vision could with the same right exclaim '*theos!*', so that we here have what are really two different ways of expressing the same experience. These moments of intensity were not merely *postulated* for men by the Greeks but were reached as a matter of historical fact, on the one hand by the religious Greek, on the other by the Greek philosopher. The convergence of the two approaches once more finds expression in the language. Philosophy, to denote the peak reached by the philosophical approach, borrowed a word from the religious sphere, where it denoted something well-known and concrete. The word was *theoria*, the name by which both these peaks of Greek religious life were called.

'Theory' has in all modern languages a sound different from that which it once had for the Greek philosophers, though it is they who were responsible for its change of meaning, in the direction of abstract thought. For the Greeks *theoria* had a double sound of 'looking' or 'viewing', from *thea*, 'spectacle', and *horan* 'to see'. The word, compounded of these two elements expresses a religious love of spectacle which was peculiar to the Greeks. The looking which is here meant is not 'looking through', it referred not to the transparency of the medium but to the primary, immediate object of vision—the forms of the gods. The Greek language of today still has no other word for paganism but the name the Christians gave it, *eidololatria* 'service of idols'. By this contemptuous simplification the ancient Christians hit on a characteristic of Greek life in its dealings with the divine. Greek religion is characterised by the worship of the visible appearances of the gods, above all by their appearance in human shape. It was served by the portraits of the gods and by an art which succeeded in giving these portraits an ever greater degree of liveliness as an enticement to worship. The word 'enticement' is here apt, for the worship was certainly no less directed to the radiance which streams out from a perfect physical appearance than to the god of whom the cult portrait was a bodily representation.

The verb *theorein* which corresponded to the substantive *theoria* can be

compared both in its fundamental meaning and in its classical and post-
classical use with the Latin *visitare*—from *video*—which has the sense of
heightened seeing and looking and corresponds originally to the institution of
the *theoros*.[207]   These official festival 'visitors' or envoys combined in their
office the two outstanding characteristics of Greek religiosity, the festive
quality and the standpoint of the onlooker.   The festival embassy itself was
called *theoria* and was sent out by a State on a 'visit of inspection', or 'spec-
tatorship'—to some distant place where a deity had once appeared to men
and where the occasion was now celebrated with a festival.   Apollo himself,
who visits his people from a distance, is in this capacity called *theorios* and
thearios.[208]   A mere delight in show-going can become a ceremonial visit
to a deity, provided only that it is combined with a fleeting prayer.   At
the beginning of Plato's *Republic* Socrates describes such a visit.   Out of
pure curiosity he went down to the Piraeus with his friends to view the
fire of the Thracian goddess, then he prayed to her, and thus returned not
from a mere sight-seeing visit, but from a *theoria*.[209]

When Aeschylus used the word *theoros* instead of *theates* (the ordinary
word for spectator) he meant a greater, more solemn spectacle.   The show
in the *theatron*, the 'place of looking on' at the Dionysus festivals, is not
called *theoria*, because it takes place in your own city.   But when the
daughters of Oceanus come as onlookers from a distance to view the
sufferings of Prometheus, they are *theoroi*.[210]   It is only with the younger
Ionians, like Herodotus and Democritus, that *theorein* and *theoria* seem to
have lost their colour, so that no special festive quality clings to them any
longer.[211]   With the Pythagorean philosopher Philolaus *theorein* refers to a
sacred thing, to Number.[212]   Plato's use of the word is no less festal.[213]
And finally there is Aristotle, who compares the *theoria* of the philosopher
not just with any vision or show, but with that of Olympia, to which
actual embassies, *theoriai*, were sent out, and with that of the Dionysus
festivals.

Independently of any relation to a cult, Aristotle finds the divine element
in *theoria*.   He connects the experience of *theorein*, of the festively enhanced
show, with the divine in man, the *nous*.   He is quite conscious of the fact
that by praising the philosophic life, the *bios theoretikos*, he is showing man
the way to godliness.[214]   They should try to be like the immortals—
athanatizein.   In this way he postulates, as a peak of Greek religious experi-

ence, something which can be reached only by philosophy. But when Aristotle wants to paraphrase this possibility of the philosophic life more exactly, he has only two analogies at his disposal, one negative and one positive. Negatively he contrasts the *bios theoretikos* with the *bios praktikos*, that form of life which is defined by utility.[215] On a blessed isle, where we have nothing else to do, this one good would still be left to us, *theoria*. *Praxis* is useful, *theoria* is good. Anyone may here perceive the contrast between the things of everyday and the festal things. Positively, we have the analogy of the festive show, at Olympia or in the theatre.

What Aristotle does not need to say is that this show, at the great Hellenic and Athenian festivals, has something divine about it. As a Greek he assumed this, though a non-Greek would hardly have recognised it. We on the other hand identified the structure of the Homeric festal world by this point, that it is a *theatron*, a show place for divine onlookers. And so we understand that in a Greek festival this situation of the *thea*, the spectacle, repeats itself. The participants are athletes, successors of the Homeric heroes, who held their competitions at the funeral games, or actors—in Tragedy performers of the heroes' parts. To such a festive show gods and men come festally, come as *theoroi*.

In the spectacle of the heroic competition, a *theoria* which is on the one hand determined by the *aidos* of those looked on at and is on the other a *sebas* for the participants, here too we encounter a peak of Greek religious experience. Not everything important has thus been said about it, yet the evident facts of Greek history, at least, have been put in the foreground of our study of Greek religion. If we do wish to characterise the Style of Greek religion by the experience which dominated it, we may call it the *Religion of Show*.

So long as the world constitutes for the Greeks a bodily and spiritual unity, the self-evident objects of the Greek Show are Forms. Ideal Forms on which the mind's eye is bent, Forms colourful and plastic in which the eyes of all Greeks delight. By once more finding the Hellenic Festal Show in this world and no longer in another world where Socrates and Plato had sought it Aristotle succeeded in restoring for later ages an originally unified world. Greek eyes remain religious even when the world has ceased to be transparent for them and when humility and resignation have taken the place of the self-assured archaic life. Menander,[216] the poet whose view of men was touched with the laughter of the gods, makes one of his heroes say:[217]

> 'The man that I
> Call happy, Parmenon, is one who takes
> A *look* at what is glorious in this world
> And quickly then returns from whence he came.
> For these, the sun which shines for all, the stars,
> The march of clouds, the sea, the gleam of fire,
> You'll still see though you live to be a hundred,
> And if you live no longer than a year
> There's nothing nobler you can see than these'.

2

RELIGIO

A simplification such as 'religion of show' only has sense if it really seizes what is essential in a Style. If we now turn to Roman religion and first of all consider it in the form of *pietas*, there is, in contrast to the Greek transparency and joy in seeing, a striking impression of something *blind*. The kind of circular motion which, as we have seen, the Roman idea of *pietas* imposes on the world has no suggestion of transparency about it, and can keep its internal consistency without the help of mental or physical vision. Vision implies distance, *pietas* nearness. The portrait of Aeneas, in whom Vergil created the ideal form of a man of *pietas*, exactly confirms this impression. He carried his father like a small child—his own—on his shoulder and saved his life, just as the daughter who was the prototype of *pietas* saved her mother's or father's life with her own milk. The invisible nearness of his gods surrounds Aeneas and creates about him an opaque atmosphere in which he moves like a blind man. He must be led—and is led. He needs signs—and gets them.

This is how the natural extension of *pietas* shows itself, as a world full of signs. Signs are not identical with symbols. Symbols in the ancient sense are abbreviations, epitomes of divine or sacred events.[218] They are clear for anyone who knows the detailed mythological story or ritual procedure of which they are an abbreviation. Signs on the other hand admit of interpretations, often have several meanings, and are always tied to the moment. Or to put it metaphorically, they are voices of the age. The continual respect for such a world of signs, unfolding itself in time, is called *religio*. It stands in the same relation to *pietas* as *theoria* to *aidos*. For the Greeks it was natural to define the pious man as 'the one who has the gods before his eyes'.[219] Cicero, in a context which according to our ideas is far removed from the religious sphere, describes the *ears* as 'religious'. He speaks of the *aures religiosae* of the Attic orators.[220]

As with the Greeks we found, in Aristotle's use of *theoria*, a tendency for two peaks of religious experience to merge in one, so with the Romans we find a similar convergence in the case of *religio*, and it is Cicero in particular whom we must consult if we want to learn something of the essence of Roman religion. This is not because of a chance phrase like *aures religiosae* above, though this does express something important about the original, not solely religious, character of the word. For though Cicero's approach is that of a philosopher, not of the simple pious folk, his religious consciousness speaks out clearly enough in the passage already quoted from his speech 'On the Diviners' Reply'. He talks of this con-sciousness, for which the Romans were indebted to the Greeks, in the Greek fashion. He records an insight such as a Greek philosopher might have had (*perspeximus*). The object of this insight, however, is specifically Roman—that everything is subject to the rule and directed by the *numen* of the gods. A Greek here instead of *numen* would have said *nous*, as we know that Anaxagoras in fact did say.[221] *Nous* has put everything in order because it knew about order, and this meant the realisation of order. *Numen* is something quite different from *Nous*. The root meaning of the word could be paraphrased somewhat as follows: to produce an effect by a sign of movement (*nutus*). Man according to Aristotle must be like the gods because he too is in possession of *nous*. No man on the other hand could claim possession of *numen*, unless perhaps by a special apotheosis of quite a different kind from that meant by Aristotle. Nor is it Aristotle from whom Cicero's way of thinking derives but Academic *skepsis*, a line of thought which runs parallel with the Aristotelian, and which means a mere human 'looking-on', a viewing with 'restraint' (*epoche*) and doubt. Here is the convergence with *religio*.

In the third book of his work 'On the nature of the gods' (*De Natura*

Deorum), Cicero chose a holder of the highest Roman priestly dignity, the Pontifex C. Aurelius Cotta, as an upholder of his own philosophical views, the views of the Academics.[222] Like Cicero himself, Cotta was faithful to the critical spirit of the later Platonic school, the so-called New Academy. The school was not dominated by any form of strict dogmatism, and the scepticism which it professed was not of a nihilistic kind. Cotta emphasises that he is interested not in refutation for its own sake but in verifying the arguments used by others. In his first book he deals critically with the Epicureans, and subjects their reasoning to close scrutiny. The Stoics are his next target. Here he makes a profession of faith which to the modern reader will appear surprising. He prefaces his sharply critical discussion with a remarkable passage which shows how much the Romans themselves knew about the peculiarity of their *religio*. Any study of Roman religious experience could take it as a starting point.

In Cicero's dialogue the Stoic who speaks before Cotta delivers a defence of the Roman State religion by interpreting it in the sense of Stoic Pantheism, and expects the Roman Pontifex thus far to agree with him. Cotta does indeed take his position as Pontifex seriously and is determined to defend the Roman religion unconditionally, in its entirety, and in all circumstances. But he does not want a defence based on interpretation, and roundly rejects the assistance of Greek philosophy. When it is a question of religion, he argues, attention must be paid not to the leaders of Stoic thought but to men who have held the highest Roman priestly dignity. He relies particularly on Laelius, who was both an augur and a philosopher, and on a famous speech in which Laelius defended the ancient aristocratic forms of the Roman cult. The fact that Laelius had been a philosopher is important to him because his example shows that the two attitudes, the augur's and the philosopher's, are compatible. Cotta's own attitude to the representative of Stoic philosophy who speaks before him is quite different from the recognition he accords to his priestly predecessors. The Stoic is required first of all to give reasons for the religion he preaches, whereas Cotta put faith in his ancestors without asking for reasons.

Modern commentators find a lack of consistency in this willingness of the philosopher-priest and so also of Cicero himself [223] to be sceptical about everything except their own religion. It was natural to compare such split thinking with that of an eighteenth-century prince of the Church, whose enlightenment and free-ranging philosophy would stop short of the actual doctrines of the Church. A general similarity cannot be denied, especially as the Ciceronian age gives evidence of other similar internal discords. None the less, we must not judge ancient paganism by Christian standards. The commentator should consider what he himself as a student of religion would do in the Academician Cotta's place. He too, when Roman religion is being discussed, must reject any Greek philosophic interpretation, especially a Stoic one. And he must put faith in the priestly authorities cited by Cotta and believe that the gods and ceremonies in their own ancient Roman world were as they described.

Neither Cotta nor the modern student of religion are here 'believers' in the Christian sense. A faith given in this way is not direct experience, not like Christian faith a victory won with God's help over doubt. Nor is it here religious faith in the sense which the word 'religious' has for us, but a substitute for such faith, an adjunct of his other beliefs. Both the academician Cotta and the historian of today stand outside that archaic Roman Existence in which Roman religion was direct experience. Even Cotta is already too far out on the boundary of that experience, he too must 'put faith' in others who were still inside it. But he can do it easily, sincerely, and without reservations. His faith in the authority of his ancestors is a natural adjunct to that religion which as a Roman is still his, but is yet no longer like a direct experience or even like an unthinking traditional acceptance. His religious attitude has one thing in common with that of the modern student of religion. Both wish to *show regard for* what is historically given and therefore *respect* it.

Cotta, the Pontifex, unintentionally fulfils one of the requirements of genuine historical research. He respectfully stops short at what is given. But he has no such respect for the Stoic *naturalis theologia*. He overthrows its proofs of the existence of God, as had already been done by the Greek masters whom Cicero follows, the great academicians Arcesilaus and Carneades. In the Academy it seems to have been an anticipation of a state of affairs which we encounter later on in the history of Christianity. The *theologia naturalis* or *rationalis* is attacked while the traditional religion is left alone. The only difference is that for the Christian his religion is derived from supernatural and non-rational guarantees, from a revelation which is not of this world.

H

From what then do we derive the religion of an Arcesilaus, who introduced the Sceptic 'restraint', the *epoche*, into the Academy at the beginning of the third century? Greek and Roman religion are founded on *this* world and belong with their *Style* to special forms of Existence, the Greek and the Roman. One religion is a pre-philosophic, and yet not unintellectual, fact of Roman history, the other of Greek history. Greek religion continues to exist as a fact alongside Greek philosophy. Arcesilaus can use the language of Greek religion to express his belief in a divine, philosophically unattainable knowledge. He does it by substituting the word *nous* for *bios* in a line of Hesiod [224]: 'The gods keep the *nous* always hidden from men'. A sentence like this is a strong confirmation of what we have already said about *nous*. If the gods did not keep it hidden, men would be like Zeus. But Arcesilaus, like Socrates in Plato's Phaedrus, saw that truth is attainable only for God, not for Man. Truth, according to the Greek meaning of *nous*, would be also supreme power. In this humility we see the kind of 'vision' which the New Academy had chosen in opposition to Aristotle. The world has become opaque. The only possibility of vision is that kind which in Greek is called *skepsis*.[225]

Thus there began a movement of Greek philosophic thought in the direction of what the Romans meant by *religio*. Aristotle started out from man's faculty for *athanatizein*, his participation in *Nous*. *Theoria*, which originally implied distance, a mere viewing of the divine forms, emerges in his individual and yet truly Greek religion as a divine victory over distance, not 'viewing' but 'touching', *thinganein*.[226] For any Greek who did not follow Aristotle but continued to feel this distance as unconquerable there was still the life of a Socrates to be lived, a tireless search for truth, with the consciousness that it was still far off. Or when one was no longer a Socrates believing himself confirmed in his mission by the Delphic god, there was human *skepsis* and human *epoche*, the withholding of judgment about a world whose divinity had lost its clearness and become invisible. Gods and *Nous* even then belonged incontestably to the Style of Greek Existence.

Carneades, who lived about a hundred years later, has made a confession of his negative dependence on the Stoa. He is said to have remarked jokingly,[227] 'If Chrysippus had not existed, I should not exist either.' Thus he defined the sense and purpose of the New Academy. Opposition to the dogmatism of the Stoics, and in Carneades' case particularly to the dogma of providence as it had been preached by Chrysippus, is our reason for the sceptical turn finally taken by the Platonic school. The attitude of not-knowing, preached by Plato as a preliminary to his doctrine of the ideas or eternal prototypes, was not only taught in the New Academy but extended to the point where even not-knowing could not be claimed with certainty. In the Stoa, whose founders and best-known teachers came from the East, the intellectual premises of Greek religion, the predilection for viewing and seeing, the joy in form and in human appearance, were no longer effective. The limits of Style within which a 'knowing vision' or a 'seeing knowledge' of the gods was possible, disappeared. The deity now could be formless, without contours, and without the intensity of a special event in which to show itself. The *theologia naturalis* and *rationalis* of the Stoa was intended to replace the real foundations, known and unknown, of the ancient religion. Its incapacity to do so was proved by the Academics in the spirit and with the weapons of Greek philosophy, while its claims to do so were rejected by Cicero on the ground of Roman tradition.

There was one line of philosophic development which came close to Roman piety, as exemplified by Cotta. The *epoche* of the Greek Academics, the withholding of judgment, corresponded to the *negative* aspect of that attitude of *carefulness* and *regard* which, in its complete form, combining the negative and positive aspects, was specifically Roman. For this the Latin language had the word *religio*. A human attitude like *religio* can never be understood from the external causes which may occasion it, but only from the human being who is capable of it. The words once addressed, with complete self-confidence, to the supreme head of a dogmatic church, that the chief thing was the *homo religiosus*,[228] showed great wisdom and a wonderful knowledge of human nature. The 'primitive' Roman, though we know nothing of him, must certainly have been a *homo religiosus* if he was the source of the religion of those priestly Romans on whom Cotta relied. The *homo religiosus* need not necessarily be the holder of a priestly office. It is wrong to think that the Greek and Roman priesthood had no spiritual basis because it rested neither on a special vocation (*vocatio*)[229] nor on special knowledge, but was attainable under certain legal conditions by every citizen. Its spiritual basis was *religio* and no less positive for the fact that everyone—or nearly everyone—had it. On the contrary, it was positive enough and rich enough in content even for the highest members of the priesthood.

This richness of content in *religio*, the *attention* and *carefulness* exercised by the Romans in all circumstances, did not necessarily mean a personal richness of religious feelings proceeding out of a man's own self. Its content was formed, not by a theory of the gods, at least not necessarily, but by the 'being' of the gods, which presupposes them and uninterruptedly affirms them in a natural, unemphatic way, just as *pietas* does. To 'be open' to the 'being' of the gods, not just physically, but also mentally — so we might paraphrase *religio*. But it would not sufficiently express its meaning. For merely to be open to the immense pressure of the gods, who laid on the Romans the burden of countless minute ceremonies and rites, would not be the same as the susceptibility which was part of *religio*. Such openness might merely mean being full of a uniform, motionless, undifferentiated substance, like a sponge in still water, or using another metaphor, a complete deafness. But this is just what we cannot say of the Romans. Their *religio* was more than merely being open, it was the complete opposite of deafness. That is why they regarded it as a special Roman aptitude, a particular faculty. It was a refined talent for listening and the continual exercise of this talent. Not a clear festive Show, not the exercise of a visual or visionary faculty, not prophetic ecstasy but an attitude for which there is no more obvious phrase than 'attentively listening in and acting accordingly'—that is *religio*. Finally there is a 'selective' element in *religio*—an operation of choosing by which it may even become creative. We shall return to this in the sixth chapter.

Apart from the Being of the gods, there are two further assumptions involved in *religio*. One is *Nous*, which according to Arcesilaus is withheld from men. For the Greek philosopher *nous* meant knowledge itself, a knowledge identical with divine being, unattainable for men, existing in its own right, continuing unshakably to be. The assumption of Roman religion was *numen*, divine causation, in which however the *nous* of the gods made itself known. This Roman *nous* was not quite like the Greek. A different aspect came to the fore—not reflection, the knowledge of being, but the *plan* and the *decision*. It is as if the religious Roman had had an original text for everything that happened—a 'text' because it could be 'uttered', if the gods, and above all Jupiter, wish it. Indeed, it already had been uttered, and so was called *fatum*, 'that which has been uttered', and *Jovis fatum*, because it was uttered by Jupiter. It was not identical with the providence (*pronoia*) of the Stoics although the Roman Stoics tried to make it so. Providence, *pro-noia*, put the emphasis on seeing and knowing, whereas in *fatum* the divine act of will was emphasised. This already uttered thing was hidden from men and was realised only gradually. Meanwhile it continued to find utterance, in signs. Alongside the being of the Gods these were the two assumptions of *religio*, first that something divine was being realised in what was happening all the time and secondly that this divine something was audible to anyone who 'listened' well.

Not to listen would actually be against *religio*. Cicero in his dialogue 'On Soothsaying'—the supplement to his 'On the Nature of the Gods'— emphasises that the ancient Romans had recourse to every kind of oracle, 'so that there might be no sign of truth neglected by them'.[230] To neglect, *negligere*, is the opposite of *religere* and *religio*.[231] On the other hand, the type of man who believes every kind of oracle unconditionally and arranges his whole life in accordance with oracles, treating them as signs of providence, is considered by Cicero not religious but *superstitiosus*, an 'enthusiast'. Cicero in this dialogue does not succeed in distinguishing clearly and unambiguously between *superstitio* and *religio*. Yet there remain certain characteristics on the one hand of the *religens*—as an old saying calls the 'religious man' [232]—and of the *superstitiosus* on the other, and these enable us to identify negative and positive aspects of the religious experience which was specifically Roman. The negative aspects were given by *superstitio*. By translating *superstitiosus* as 'enthusiast' I mean to stress the view that it was the Latin translation of the Greek *ekstasis*.[233] Its use in the sense of the modern 'superstition' and 'superstitious' is in keeping with the Roman condemnation of all enthusiasm, indeed any form of exaggeration in the religious sphere. As an exaggeration of *religio*, *superstitio* meant to be helplessly subservient to signs and to think them always and everywhere as referring to oneself. Positive, genuine *religio* by contrast kept within bounds, like *eulabeia*. It was to be absolutely open to divine world events, to listen acutely for signals and to direct one's life accordingly.

The Style is just as evident here as in that aspect of Greek religious experience which was indicated by the word *theoria*. The essence of Greek Style was there summed up in the simple phrase 'Religion of Show'. The essence of *religio*, by contrast, the fundamental characteristic of Roman religion, can scarcely be comprehended in one word. It is an attitude of listening, open to every sign and continually adjusting itself to them. A further difference is that *religio* does not possess a clear, festal quality like *theoria*. It is in some sense fulfilment, but only as given by a universal prudence and reserve or by the general susceptibility to signs, which almost all the peoples of the ancient world possessed to some extent. *Religio* is scarcely to be compared with a single 'peak experience' like the 'vision of the gods' in its two meanings of seeing the gods and seeing like the gods. Rather it is like a line running at a constant level, on which *religio* is *potentially* present everywhere, as a simple, worshipping openness. When it is *actually* present, when, as the Romans say, *religio est*, then we have a special condition which presents the greatest possible contrast to the festive quality —the condition of the *dies religiosi*. On such days everything has regard only for the divine, tries to recover its adjustment to the divine, to atone for any deviation from the 'line' of *religio*. Just as the great Agonistic festivals were an objective form of appearance of the Show of the Gods, so one may consider the whole course of Roman history as an objective realisation of *religio*.[234]

Our attempt to define the Style of Greek and Roman religious experience and its 'peaks' must necessarily lead us into the wider regions of Greek and Roman *Existence*, the Greek and Roman *bios*, and must necessarily be confronted in either case by that which constitutes the essence of these two forms of existence. In Greece it was the Show which included not only religion but also philosophy and art, in Rome the ability to follow *fatum* in the course of a duller, less philosophic, and less artistic life and yet a life of listening and obeying, a life of compliance. What we now have to do is to turn from the general to the special, from the most extensive to the most concrete, the 'form' of the Greek and of the Roman cult. From these forms we here need to seize only the principal element, the Greek and Roman fashion of relating man to god.

DELOS and BRAURON

and the cults of Apollo and Artemis

67 *Delos: a bird's-eye view of the site*

68 *Delos: one of the lions*

69 *The sacred way of Delos with the lions. 6th century B.C.*

70 *Apollo with deer, from Tomb 559 in the Valle Trebba, Spina. Archaeological Museum, Ferrara*

71 *Apollo pours a libation for Artemis. Vase by the Bologna painter, c. 455 B.C.*
From Tomb 308 in the Valle Trebba, Spina. Archaeological Museum, Ferrara

72 *Ruins of the Temple of Artemis at Brauron*

73 *Early statue of Artemis from Brauron. National Museum, Athens*

74 *Early statue of Artemis seated, from Brauron. National Museum, Athens*

75 Statue of a young girl,
one of the 'bears' of Artemis,
from Brauron.
National Museum, Athens

76 Portrait heads of young girls, called the 'bears', from Brauron. National Museum, Athens

77 *Bas-relief of Artemis with hind and adorants, from Brauron. Late 5th century B.C. National Museum, Athens*

79 *Bas-relief of Zeus, Leto, Apollo, Artemis, awaiting a host of adorants, from Brauron. National Museum, Athens*

Bas-relief of a procession of adorants sacrificing to Artemis, from Brauron. National Museum, Athens

Bas-relief of Artemis with goat and kids, from Brauron

81 *Frieze from the Villa of the Mysteries, Pompeii. Mid-1st century B.C*

CHAPTER V

Man and God according to Homer and Hesiod

I

THE GREEK IDEA OF THE SACRIFICE

THE GREEK AND THE ROMAN types of religious experience are both, in their own Style, phenomena of the history of man, objective realities which once existed in their own right, whether or not we succeed in describing them correctly. They do have their subjective aspect, but this is never adequate to define them. Greek religious experience is not merely *sebas* and *aidos*, two words which indicate subjective feelings. For these feelings were an accompaniment to a particular kind of imaginative representation, in which one particular aspect of the world's potential variety became actual. The world of men can really show itself in a variety of different ways, and in no other religion did the world show its abundance of Forms as it did through Greek religious experience. The case is similar with Roman religious experience. *Religio* too is associated with a special kind of representation, in which another of the world's potential aspects is made to give an actual manifestation of its presence.

Representation, the making present of what was remote, what was thought of as possible but was not yet real and actual, this is a creative act. Man and the world take part in it together. It happens in works of art or in the experiences of religion and the works which result from them. And none of it can happen without Style. We are here speaking of two modes of representation, as different from one another as are the Greek and the Roman Style. To the Greek Style there correspond bodily manifestations of gods to which the poetry and art of the sculptors and painters powerfully contributed. From later times we have accounts of epiphanies, stories in which the gods were awake and frequently showed themselves to dreaming men.[235] There is no evidence of anything in these epiphanies

I

which might be regarded as a breach of the Style appropriate to the art in which they are commemorated. Divine appearances in their truest Greek form are marked by an intellectual and at the same time sculptural clarity, an *enargeia*, and with that by an aptitude for 'viewing knowledge' which found its greatest fulfilment among the poets and artists. The Roman mode of representation, on the other hand, implies the passage of the world's time. Yet this passage of time itself has two ways of revealing its actual presence, ways in which man himself is passive but yet not absent.

One of these ways is given by the recurring phases of time. In its periodical course time passes through regular peaks at which it is festal, that is, more present. I used this paraphrase for the festive quality earlier on, when I had not yet come to speak of different kinds of representation, or looking at it objectively, of the world's presence. From this point of view time appears as a series of festival years, or longer festival periods like the Greek Olympiads. This time becomes the content of Calendars, and 'the Calendar is essentially a Festival Calendar'.[236] The refined aptitude of the Romans to which they gave the name *religio* is matched by the refined elaboration of the Roman Calendar. The Roman way is here distinguished from the Greek only by a difference of emphasis, a different choice of what is important. The festival time-phases constitute points of contact between the Roman and Greek Styles. As phases of *time* they have their temporal aspect. As *phases*, a word which originally meant the *phaseis*, or 'appearances', of constellations in ancient astronomy, they imply also a standing still of time, not in the mystical [237] but in the intellectual sense, not as an eternity '*dove s'appunta ogni ubi ed ogni quando*', but as a point from which clear Forms become visible to the mind's eye outside 'every where and every when'. The Roman has a greater preference than the Greek for giving objective expression to something which appears in the passage of time. The life of the *Flamen Dialis* will serve us as an example. The Greek demand is more for a festival phase which ensures that time is worthily represented even when its passage is felt in Roman fashion. It is the essence of the feast that it is, so to speak, a standstill in the world's course, a moment at which eternal Forms may show themselves and by showing themselves extend it to a motionless eternity.

Another way for time to become more present than normal is given, as we have already said, by the *dies religiosi*. These are festive in a negative sense. What is characteristically Roman is that such days are not only observed—the Greeks regularly accepted such unlucky days, as for instance the fifth day of the month in Hesiod [238]—but when specially unlucky are even taken into the Calendar. For the Greeks such days are there, so to speak, to provide a regular representation of the harmful and lethal realities of the world. The Romans on such days commemorate the possibility of a disturbance of their good relationship with the gods, the *pax et venia deum*. For them such days are historical warnings not to deviate from the way partly prescribed in the Festival Calendar. To them every way was not periodically closed, but open to the future, just as the world itself is open in the passage of time. The openness of *religio* is matched by this openness of the world. For that reason *religio* is more than the observance of temporal obligations which can be fixed in time. *Religio* also includes another faculty, that of perceiving as a divine gesture something which is not fixed but only becomes present in the moment, and of fulfilling it accordingly.

Not every representation of the deity can be called a cult, in the narrower sense of the word, though in the wider sense it was always natural to regard the representation of the divine in the works of poets and artists as a kind of 'cult'. The oldest sources which have anything to tell us, directly or indirectly, about Greek religion, in connected texts that is, and not just in the form of lists or fragments, are poetic works. There is one question we cannot avoid. How is the divine in its relation to men represented in the works which have been transmitted to us under the names of Homer and Hesiod? Both were regarded by the Greeks as authorities on religion, almost as religious founders or at least as arrangers and interpreters of the world of gods. The first historic surmise about the origin of Greek religion in the form in which it was generally valid in Greece and later became known as classical comes from Herodotus.[239] According to the 'father of history' it was Hesiod and Homer who gave the Hellenes a doctrine about the origin of the gods, gave the gods themselves their appellations, defined their 'offices', their spheres of sovereignty, and described their natures and Forms (*eidea*). The way in which Homer introduces the gods in the Iliad allows us a glimpse of the age which came before this poem.

From the fifteenth century onward, when the names of Greek gods occur in the written records of Cretan and Mycenean palaces, first at Cnossus, then at Pylos and Mycenae itself, there was a lapse of at least six centuries before Homer.[240]   Yet every step we take into the pre-Homeric period for the present requires a special scrutiny.[241]   It is becoming more and more possible, however, to distinguish a pre-Homeric Style in Greek religion. Most of what lived on into later times and determined Greek Existence, alongside, or to some extent in opposition to, Homer, was associated with the name Dionysus, a great god of the pre-Homeric and post-Homeric age.[242] At the Dionysiac festivals the whole of Greek life became more agitated. Yet these agitations too fit into one great context in which the ruler was not Dionysus but Zeus.   Even the greatest of all Dionysiac events, the reappearance of the ancestors from the kingdom of the dead, so that they may 'be viewed' in the theatre,[243] took place in the Style of general Greek religious experience and the appearing ghosts assumed the shapes in which they had emerged from the Epic poems.   Still, the presence of Dionysus was demonstrated not only by the celebrations in which the dead awoke, like the Anthesteria and the great Dionysia at Athens, or by the periodical drunken occasions, or by states of ecstasy to which the women surrendered themselves, at greater intervals, in the special Dionysiac women's festivals, but also continuously by the vine and its products, in all phases of its growth into fruit and manufacture into wine.   And so one piece of Nature under a special name became a common foundation for all the great cultures about the Mediterranean.   As with corn, the element of Demeter, so with the fundamental Dionysiac element a piece of Nature entered at all times and everywhere into the Style of those cultures which were built upon it. The natural foundation is always taken for granted, however much the radiance of the divine may rest upon it.   Homer took the vine as a matter of course but regarded it as less divine than the figures which gathered on his Olympus.   To be concerned with it was for him the business of peasants or, in the prescribed manner, of women.   Homer seldom mentioned Dionysus by name, though he existed for him no less than the other gods.

There is one way of representing the divine which comes closest to expressing the religious experience of the average ancient man.   This is always the cult in its narrowest sense.   Conversely, a cult which represented nothing and wanted only to cast a wish, so to speak, into a godless world, to cast it out into the unknown, would not be a cult.   Even if we chose to start from the supposition that cults originally created their own gods, we should still have to suppose that each cult had an object of which it was a representation—in this case the god created by the cult. Cults which are merely magical performances make an effort to represent the performers themselves as divine. And the cult is *primarily* representation, and only secondarily a request and a gift [244] to one who is represented. Examples which point unambiguously in this direction can easily be found in the Greek cult as known to history. The cult performance at Tanagra, as described by Pausanias and interpreted by Walter F. Otto,[245] is particularly clear. At a festival of Hermes the best-looking of the young men walked round the city with a ram on his shoulders. He did this as one who was deputising for the god through his own bodily appearance. According to the tradition at Tanagra this performance commemorated an epiphany of Hermes. Though the ceremony was intended to serve also as a preventive against epidemics, its primary significance is clear—representation. There were also less transparent representations, like the leap from the Leukas Rock, a leap which originally only a god could make, while the man who performed it often lost his life in the act.[246]

Such actions were repetitions of mythological events, stories of gods which were abbreviated to ritual gestures,[247] but which the drama of the ceremony made more present to those taking part than mere narrations would have done. In the intensity of the representation the cult dominated the myth and even caused it to be forgotten. The more detailed the ceremony still was, the more the original myth shone through it. Thus it was with the bull sacrifice when performed with the archaic elaboration of the Bouphonia at Athens.[248] But what about the sacrifice of 'a hundred cattle', a 'hecatomb', even several hecatombs, which in its quantitative exaggeration was rather the reverse of elaborate? The Homeric descriptions of the ceremony of sacrifice leave us in no doubt that the really festive part of the business was the slaughtering of the animal and its preparation as food. There was something divine about this event, something which had at the same time a life-giving and a death-dealing aspect. When women were present at the ceremony, they shrieked aloud at the moment when the sacrificial animal received the blow.[249] This belonged to the rite of the ox-sacrifice, but was none the less a direct, natural utterance, like the symbolic action of Hecuba in Book XXII of the Iliad. A cry uttered by women when they saw an event of death before their eyes does not have to be explained in terms of a special purpose. Perhaps they were driving off ghosts? No, the sort of ghosts known to the archaic Greek religion, such as the Harpies, could not have been so easily driven off. Or perhaps it was even a cry of joy, lamentations being forbidden in a holy place? [250] Such speculations only take us further and further away from the reality. Of course it is not lamentation which rings out at the climax of the whole sacrificial act. There is joy in it among other things, joy in a feast of nature, but contradictory like nature itself, Fundamentally what is heard here is a natural awe of that which is made present in the feast. Food springs forth from the death of noble creatures, who themselves stand under the protection of the gods, and in the archaic period are also akin to them—thus we may paraphrase the divine event which was brought about by the great cattle sacrifices of the Greeks.

This is confirmed by very ancient customs connected with the killing of cattle which have been preserved outside the Homeric poems.[251] The ceremony of the Athenian *bouphonia* is a clear enough indication of the murder aspect of the cattle killing. The Greeks themselves explained the holiness of cattle by reference to their idea that all cultivation of the soil was a domain of holiness presided over by the goddess Demeter. The plough animals were objects of respect and loving care.[252] We find our-selves here in the primitive Mediterranean world and not far removed from those cultures in which the cow and the ox were holy animals and a form of appearance of the divine. For us, however, in order to understand the naturally festive character of the cattle-killing, it is enough to visualise the aspect assumed by this animal in the dominions of Demeter. This aspect is Greek and not entirely absent from the world of Homer, although in the Homeric poems it remains in the background. That which feeds us and is itself also food, so we might describe it, that which gives food and must be killed in order to become food. In this the cow and the ox are kin to Demeter's fruit, the corn which must similarly be mown to the ground. It is known that corn too has an inherently festive character which was long preserved.

The slain animal was not thought of as an individual any more than the mown corn. It was always the whole race which suffered in it, which laboured, died, and became food.[253] Nor was the slain animal identical, in Demeter's domain, with the goddess herself. It was not even her form of

82 Nemesis, 'daughter of Night, the cause of much sorrow to men' (see p. 121).
Relief with a representation of the Nemesis Regina. Middle of the 2nd century A.D.
Brindisi Museum

83 *Youths with bulls and sacrificial objects dedicated to Apollo. By the Kleophon painter;
from Tomb 57c in the Valle Pega, Spina. Archaeological Museum, Ferrara*

84 *Mithras killing the bull* (see p. 187). *Vatican Museum*

85 *Athletes preparing for the torch race. Vase from Tomb 563 in the Valle Trebba, Spina. c. 420–410 B.C. Archaeological Museum, Ferrara*

appearance, as elsewhere for instance the cow is the form of appearance of the moon goddess or of great moon-like goddesses. As a participant in the cultivation of the fields it stands close to her and under her protection. Yet even when great gods like Zeus or Poseidon, not to mention Dionysus, appear in bull form, the cattle species is singled out, as sacrificial animal, for unique suffering—the suffering imposed by the gods' bounty to men. As participant in the cultivation of the fields and as food it belongs to the world domain of Demeter. One particularly clear example of this was to be found in the central miracle of a religion which was a close neighbour of the Mediterranean group—the bull-killing of Mithras. According to the myth of the Persian religion the fruit of the earth is actually identical with the sacrificed primeval bull, for corn comes out of its entrails.[254]

Greek religion with its sense of reality did not make this kind of identification. It contented itself with kinship. It incorporated the cow or ox as sacrificial animal and the fruit of Demeter, the sacrificial barley, in a single ceremonial structure, that which is common to all the great sacrifices. Homer treats the ritual details of the preliminary sacrifice less fully than the main act, the killing of the animal. One part of the preliminaries, however, he does emphasise, the scattering about the victim of special grain, the *oulai* or *oulochytai*, that is barley specially bruised for the sacrifice.[255] In this barley, the material of the preliminary sacrifice, the same divine aspect of the world was present as in the principal material, the sacrificial animal itself. This was the aspect of food. As we saw among the Australian aboriginals,[256] one can be intoxicated by this aspect of the world and represent it in cult dances. We saw how it there became festal, that is wholly present, with its face of life and its face of death, and the whole dark background of death.

In the foreground is the sacrificial meal. This is the fulfilment of the sacrifice. We have learnt to know the natural festivity which resides in every banquet. All over the world a banquet is festive, though by itself alone, at least in the ancient world, not yet a feast. For its own sake a banquet, so to speak, positively demands the presence of the gods, even when the meal is not a real sacrificial one. The gods are called upon and receive their share.[257] Everywhere in the ancient world it is difficult to distinguish between the sacrificial meal and an ordinary banquet. From what we know about the historical period we have to suppose that every slaughtered animal was actually regarded as a sacrificial animal and treated accordingly.[258]

And there is no doubt at all that this was so on State occasions and in the life of the heroic period as depicted by Homer. Great meals in the Iliad are 'meals of the gods'. A divine presence is part of the whole *idea* of the sacrificial meal. It is a presence which goes beyond the mere divinity of food and drink, and is more spiritual.

At a festive meal man and god are present to one another, in the Greek sense 'knowing of' one another. This is the fundamental idea of the Greek cult. The memorials of Greek religion, both literary and epigraphic, are full of appeals—invitations and summonses—to the gods, of songs of invitation, and songs of advent which celebrate their coming.[259] Besides the sacrificial meals there were also special entertainments carried out with all the symbols of hospitality—*theoxenia* and *theodaisia*—for wandering or distant gods, like the Dioscuri, Aesculapius, or Apollo who in this respect was also called *Theoxenios*. This phenomenon may be contrasted with the omni-presence of god among the Israelites. 'Am I a God at hand, saith the Lord, and not a God afar off? . . . Do not I fill heaven and earth, saith the Lord?'.[260] The prophet thus consciously distinguishes his God from the gods of the other ancient oriental religions which are closer to the Greek gods. His last question is unintentionally apt in the context of the Greek sacrificial rite, one special feature of which was that the animal was lifted from the earth so that it was no longer touching it when the sacrifice was offered to the high gods of Heaven and Olympus, and pressed to the earth when it was to the underworld gods or the dead.[261]

The Greek gods in this behaviour to the world are different from the God of the Israelites. Their movements are extensively bound up with the movements of the heavens. It is false to explain their comings and goings by saying that their spheres of influence are limited in space and tied to their cult sites. Every cult-place was situated in the centre of the round world and every Greek sanctuary *was* a natural sactuary. Not only in its relation to the landscape, when the place of sacrifice lay outside the city, but in relation to one of the two hemispheres, either to the upper one, the heavens, or the lower one, the underworld. This was shown by the position of the altar, which still remained in the open air even when a temple had been added to the site. An *eschara*, an altar for the underworld deities, had its connection with these deities everywhere. Every Greek place of sacrifice was waiting for the advent of the deity, unless he or she was already present. When a

Greek addressed a summons to his gods and they came in answer to it, it was because they were able to *be in any place where* they were expected, not because their power was limited to a particular place. Not only is there no traditional support for such an idea, but it is indeed unthinkable. On the other hand they may perhaps have been limited in the *time* when they might appear. There were among the gods those who had the *special* character of being 'the far god' or 'the arriving god'.[262] What is characteristic of the Greek religion is not the place relationship of its gods with men but the fact that it *could be entirely suspended*, so as to make their meeting possible.

Did the Greeks of the historical period ever really experience such meetings? This question has two answers. The first is that of the religious man of all periods, which was given by Walter F. Otto:[263] 'There is only one experience which could open our eyes and which it would be presumption even to hope for. It would be if we could feel what it means for a god to be in our immediate neighbourhood.' The other answer was given by the Greeks in their myth about the performer of the first sacrifice, who was himself a god but as representative of men slaughtered the sacrificial animal for a common meal with the gods—the myth of Prometheus, which is at the same time the myth of human existence, of the distance between gods and men.[264] After Prometheus had cheated the gods, by keeping the best parts of the victim for men, though the ceremony of sacrifice always continued to be valid for the Greeks, the gods could never again appear at it in earnest, but at most in play or in appearance. Yet this myth too assumes the idea of the meeting. It was in harmony with the Style of Greek religious experience that the gods in the festive atmosphere of cult and of poetry could mix with men.

The idea of the Greek sacrifice could only be realised by a *completely* clear epiphany and a *real* meeting with the gods. The nearness to the gods experienced by the Greeks in Homeric times and right into the modern period was not a real meeting, yet the idea was always present to the Greek mind. Such meetings with the gods at the sacrificial meal were experienced in complete clarity only by those peoples—as Homer knew—whose Existence fluctuated between divinity and humanity, who were indeed closer to the gods than to men—the Ethiopians and the Phaeacians.[265] Their King Alcinous says of the Phaeacians: 'For the gods, at least until now, always appear clearly to us when we sacrifice glorious hecatombs and they banquet with us, sitting where we sit.' The idea of the meeting with the gods—as an idea which was once realised in an ideal Existence and is realised no more —could hardly be more sharply and clearly expressed. Such an Existence is a fundamental spiritual reality of the Greek nature. It is complementary to it, and even contrasted with it in the consciousness of a great poet. But it was not by any means only Homer who thought like this. The religions of archaic peoples like to give reasons for their cult procedures in the form that these were introduced in primeval times, when gods and men had immediate intercourse with one another. This idea may be regarded as an explanation of the whole of Greek religion in its mythological character. In the spirit of the feast a religious idea like that of the sacrifice so to speak flares up and takes on time and substance. Meanwhile the same festive spirit is separated off from the passage of time and change, to become a special kind of time, primordial time.

The golden shine of festivity which for Pindar still clung to the branches carried by the victors in the festival games and transformed them to golden boughs [266] also converted this primordial time to a Golden Age. Similarly the ideas which men of the historical period tried to realise through the cult were converted to realities of the Golden Age. The Phaeacian condition described by Alcinous appears in Hesiod as the condition of the whole world in that happy period. It has been transmitted, to us as to the Greeks, as a bare quotation without context, a condition of man which must always have seemed to be the prototype of the *Theoxenia*—the Greek festival at which the gods themselves were guests. In an excellent work on Hesiod it was described as the 'primal phenomenon of Greek cult feeling' and 'as such not capable of logical analysis'.[267] 'They took their meals in those days in common, and the places at table were common to mortal men and immortal gods'—so Hesiod has it.

The idea of the meeting of man with the deity appears also in a mystical form. Absolutely, it is called the *henosis*, the 'being one'. In later Antiquity the different mystical versions are better known than the non-mystical meeting with the gods. In the text I have quoted we find this latter in absolute purity. Starting from Homer and Hesiod it can be slightly paraphrased: to sit together, and to have seeing knowledge of one another in the primal condition of being. This would be a quite general expression for it. As a general idea it can also be expressed in non-Greek terms. Apart from numberless examples from the so-called nature religions it appears among the Israelites as the visit of God and his two angels to Abraham in the plains of Mamre.[268]   The absolute form is expressed in Greek by Homer as the condition of the Ethiopians and Phaeacians, and in Hesiod as the condition described in the fragment about the common meals of gods and men. It lives on as the idea of the hearth and table fellowship of all divine beings among men and 'of the other immortals' in the archaic philosophy and in the hero cult.   Here it is the actual happening which 'unites the departed hero with the gods as with his race in indestructible communion'.   A classical expression of its other aspect is to be found in the last verse of Vergil's Fourth Eclogue, where it is said of the non-divine man,

nec deus hunc mensa, dea nec dignata cubili est

(him no god has honoured with his table nor goddess with her bed).

Such a form certainly does not admit of logical analysis.   It can, however, be traced back to its assumptions, to the idea from which it derives.   This idea, which is fundamental not only to the Greek cult but also to the Greek religion and to Greek Existence, is expounded by Hesiod himself.   It is included as a fundamental idea in the idea of the Golden Age.   For Hesiod the myth of the Golden Age was simply an assertion of this other idea.   He speaks of the Golden Age in two forms.   Either it is an initial condition with no special name, in which human and divine Existence were not yet separated, or it is an exactly delimited Age which could not be better named than after the metal gold.   It was followed by the less precious Ages of decadence —with the exception of the entirely peculiar and unique Greek Age of Heroes.   This doctrine of Ages, which Hesiod took over from the Orient,[269] is expounded by him in his *Works and Days*.   In it the 'Golden Race of Men' was also a creation of the Olympic gods.   Yet he introduces his account of this race with a clear formulation of another idea implicit in the idea of the Golden Age,[270] that 'gods and mortal men are of the same origin'.

The apparent inconsequence is here a sure sign that we have to do with the original text:[271] no one would make an interpolation contradicting the whole of what followed it.   The hard directness of the sentence, however, is also an indication that the idea it contains was really self-evident for the Greeks, so self-evident that we can call it a fundamental idea of the Greek religion.   Pindar said the same:[272] 'The race of men and gods is one.   From one mother do we draw our breath.'   Hesiod nowhere speaks of a first man, although primal men were known to Greek mythology [273] and he himself twice describes the creation of the primal woman. Where he is propounding the doctrine of the Ages, which assumes the creation of the particular 'race' identical with each such Age, he tells of a race of men which was formed of the stuff of ash trees and which fitted the Bronze Age [274] as the ashen shaft of a spear fits the bronze head. Elsewhere the human race is for him identical with the Ash-Tree Race.[275] The ash-trees were generated in the earth from the drops of the blood of Uranus as divine beings—nymphs called ash-trees —at the same time as their siblings the Erinyes ('Furies') and Giants.[276] Of the same origin as the gods, who are similarly offspring of Uranus and Gaia, Heaven and Earth, and yet a much darker race—that is what men are. The human race, on the other hand, is not doomed to destruction like the race of Giants.[277] Only Zeus could destroy it, but he does not do so, since Prometheus' theft of fire for men. There is no contradiction here with Hesiod's doctrine of the Ages of the World. For even he wants to go on living after the last Race; evidently because the great cycle of the Races will begin again.[278] This idea of humanity, of its sibling relationship to the godhead, is assumed by the idea of the Greek sacrifice and its fulfilment there.

2

THE LAUGHTER OF THE GODS

The Greek idea of the sacrifice has given us one view of the manner in which the Greeks understood the relation between man and god. A different view is given us by the laughter of the gods. Here we must first except the malicious laughter of Zeus at the end of his contest with Prometheus, as the story is told in *Works and Days*. Hesiod's narrative is based on the difference between the *Nous* of Zeus and the Titanic cast of mind of Prometheus. With Zeus the *Nous* shows itself pure and perfect, and is thus calm and motionless, like a mirror. It discovers everything without seeking, indeed everything discovers itself to it. The Titan's mind, on the other hand, is restless, inventive, and, with foreknowledge and sagacity, always on the search for something. The object of *nous* is what really *is*. The object of the Titanic intelligence is *invention*, even if only an artful lie, a deception which the gods themselves admire and are entertained by. Corresponding to *nous* is *aletheia*, the Greek 'truth', to be paraphrased as 'absence of concealment', which is actually the etymological meaning of the word.[279] The word has the sound of the denial of concealment and forgetting, of *lethe*. The Titanic intelligence loves what is 'crooked', and the epithet of Cronos in Hesiod [280] is derived from that. The lie is 'crooked' by nature, but so too is a clever invention, like the noose, which in Greek is so-called.[281]

The necessary complement of *nous* is being. When the *nous* is extinguished, being remains blind. The necessary complement of the Titanic intelligence is intellectual and general misery—stupidity, thoughtlessness, clumsiness. Each of Prometheus' inventions leaves behind it a trail of new misery for men. After his successful trick over the sacrifice, Zeus takes fire away from men. And when, after he had managed to steal back the fire, Prometheus himself was taken away from men to suffer punishment, Epimetheus was left as the representative of men—instead of the crafty one, as his complement the stupid one. The profound relatedness of these two figures is expressed in the idea that they were brothers. We might say that a single crafty and stupid being is here resolved into two persons.[282] Prometheus is the one with forethought, Epimetheus the one whose afterthought comes too late. It is he who in his thoughtlessness receives as a gift from the gods the last inexhaustible source of misery for mankind, Pandora. And as Hesiod tells us the story of this last act in the competition between the two kinds of intellect, Zeus, who has seeing knowledge of the fact that men will be entertained by the woman Pandora and love their own misfortune, laughs aloud.[283]

But elsewhere too the Greek gods laugh, and laugh differently. The famous 'Homeric laughter' is their laughter, and they laugh at their own kind. Most commentators have found this so strange that they have denied all religious meaning to Homer's scenes of divine life. Such scenes have been interpreted as creations of a mind become more or less irreligious or of a wholly non-religious mind.[284] This is completely contradicted by the attitude of the Greeks themselves, who held Homer responsible for the form of their religion, whether they did so negatively like Xenophanes or positively like Herodotus. However, it is evident that a phenomenon which impresses

K

us as so strange ought first to be understood as *characteristic*, regardless of whether it strikes us today as religious or irreligious.

The characteristic element becomes particularly clear when the laughter of Zeus, who sees the nature of men and foresees its consequences, is compared with situations in other religions in which god and man confront one another. In order to understand that specific form of the divine which is above all characteristic of the Israelite religion, we may quote the words of Abraham, in his converse with the Lord about the fate of the men of Sodom. 'Behold now, I have taken upon me to speak unto the Lord, which am but dust and ashes.'[285] Thus Abraham declares the nature of men, corresponding to a special form of the divine as it affects the feelings of men.[286] This form appears against the Sodomites as a destroying fire. Fire and ashes or dust (dry earth of which the first man was made) correspond to one another. The fire is not God but a simile to express God's relations with men, as dust and ashes are a simile of man in relation to God. Fire is the anger of God of which His creature has knowledge through the feeling of its own 'destruction'.

In comparison with this, the idea of the gods' superior laughter is no less entitled to be considered religious. The comparison also shows how characteristic it is of Greek religion. There is this characteristic difference. In the Jewish Israelite religious experience God's anger stands over against His creature's feeling of its own destruction, feeling against feeling. There can, however, stand on the one hand not anger but God's love for man— as it does overwhelmingly in the religion of Christ—and on the other again the feeling of man's own destruction—in face of so great a love! Compared with this the Greek religion must appear as without feeling. With the Greeks idea confronts idea. Hesiod expounds the idea which corresponds to the laughter of Zeus, the idea of the contradictoriness of human existence, in which men are entertained by their own ruin and love their own misfortune. In the oriental religions there is a murderously fatal,[287] an 'abysmal',[288] and also a creative laughter of the deity.[289] The laughter of Zeus is perhaps destructive, yet nobody dies *of it*. By this laughter nothing is changed in contradictory human existence, which both Prometheus and Epimetheus are equally entitled to represent. What is destroyed by this laughter? The importance of the whole Titanic misery, which was expressed by the figures of *both* Titans together. Before the angry Jehovah all creatures turn to ashes. Before Zeus, the laughing onlooker, the eternal human race plays its eternal human comedy.

Would this have been endurable, if the Greeks had always viewed their existence in such a way? Assuredly not, had not the gods also been the bountifully giving ones. What was expected of them was not election or love but friendship and abundance, the very things which it was the idea of the Greek sacrifice in its fulfilment to bring about, so far as possible through the actual feast of sacrifice. The word *philos*, which occurs in compounds with *theos*, is nearest to 'friend'. Man with his contradictions could seem altogether comic to the gods. From Zeus's point of view there showed through humanity the behaviour of crafty and stupid Titans. Yet ordinary mortals in Greece were glad to partake of this kind of nature, although for Greek sensibilities it bordered on the comic. There were others who wore this nature, less crafty beings, the Sileni and the Satyrs, the wildness of whose way of life did not mean unhappiness. But to be the unfortunate sister-race of the gods—this Greek idea of humanity is in its essence tragic. Tragic because of its kinship with the gods. 'From one mother both are sprung' said Pindar of the human and divine race. 'Yet we are separated' he continues 'by the whole division of powers so that here is nothing, while there stands a secure seat of adamant, the heavens.' Such separation, simply because it is separation, the result of a primeval division and decision, is more than painful—it is tragic. This tragic character with Pindar still has its peculiarly Greek form of polarity—on the one hand . . . on the other. . . . On the one hand he knows humanity with Apollo-like clarity as a nothing. On the other, since mankind is bound by ties of brotherhood to the gods, he sees it touched by the radiance of Zeus and celebrates that vision of the heroic Existence which is afforded by the spectacles of the great Agonistic festivals. To the Greek idea of mankind there belongs not only the half Titanic, half Silenic, comic aspect, but also the heroic aspect. And it is here that the kinship with the gods becomes most clearly evident.

Just as the Titanic and Silenic nature of man is the seat of the comic, so his heroic nature is the seat of the tragic. If the Greek idea of humanity derives its tragic aspect from the brotherhood of men and gods, it must be most purely tragic where that kinship is most purely realised—in the hero. According to Hesiod the heroes are 'demi-gods', their race, to which Hesiod has assigned a special Age, is 'a divine race'.[290] In Achilles, who in Homer represents the hero in his purest form, the polarity of nothingness and divinity are blended into a single destiny. Achilles is a demi-god, the son of a goddess. Other heroes only have the mist snatched from before their eyes in a rare moment, only exceptionally are they granted clear vision, like Diomedes in the press of battle, in which he is allowed to see the gods, or Hector, when he foresees the end of Troy and the house of Priam. Achilles through his mother has his eyes open to that which is hidden from ordinary men. He chooses with open eyes the nothingness of human existence when he walks into the chain of consequences provoked by Epimethean actions—the actions of Patroclus and Hector. He chooses destruction. Not in order to give divinity to human nothingness, but to preserve his own image, of which the hero's loyalty to his squire forms part. With *such* a death self-chosen, he cannot be otherwise than the hero! It is a simplification, but not one contrary to the spirit of Homer, to say that the world in the Iliad takes on a heroic aspect pre-eminently because of this destruction chosen with open eyes.[291]

This heroic world depicted for us by Homer honours the gods with sacrifices, sacrifices according to a Promethean rite inherited from a still more ancient world, but which the poet has brought as near as he could to the pure idea of the Greek sacrifice. But over *this* world, too, the laughter of the gods resounds. What is the meaning of their laughter in relation to the tragic aspect of the idea of humanity? They do not laugh because of some intention of the poet, but with the most natural spontaneity. Nor do they laugh over the fate of the heroes, although these heroes are not at all free from human contradictions! Zeus least of all laughs at them, for it is he would so gladly save Hector from the death that is the consequence of his Epimethean action.[292] When there is something destructive in Zeus's laughter, this in Homer is not directed against mankind, and this is especially not the case with the puzzling laughter of Zeus in Book XXI of the Iliad. And yet this laughter has its meaning in relation to tragic mankind, just as in Hesiod it had its meaning in relation to comic mankind.

The scenes in which the gods laugh in Homer are not burlesque and in no way detract from the perfection of the divine image. Certainly their laughter clings to them. They are both laughers and laughed at. It is this laughter of the gods among themselves which is so strange and calls for an effort of understanding. One such attempt was based on Schelling's philosophy of art. It asserted that the laughter of the gods gave a sharper and clearer outline to their image. They had to laugh, as it were, in order to appear more themselves. Image, or form, meant limitation and limitation meant something finite. Laughter, however, 'eternally dances attendance on the spiritually finite. . . . And even an angel is laughable—for an archangel'.²⁹³ That is why the Homeric gods, too, become laughable when they reach the limits of their suzerainty and their power. It is in the contact between finite and infinite, according to this explanation, that laughter rings out.²⁹⁴ This seems to be particularly apt when Hephaestus, for instance, in Book I of the Iliad plays the part of Ganymede.²⁹⁵ The god himself seems here consciously to avail himself of the aesthetic recipe, that a violation of the limits of one's own form arouses laughter. Even if Homer's art was not so conscious as all that, we cannot but admire it. But he has also depicted the *form* of the god in the same way. The actual figure of the smith-god emerges all the more clearly by an effect of contrast, from the comparison with the lovely Ganymede. But is not this figure distinct in general from those of the Olympian gods?

This is not a question of forms which can only be judged aesthetically but of the actual difference between gods and Titans. This manual worker among the gods is fundamentally a Titanic form, in his nature and in his cult close to Prometheus.²⁹⁶ The first and most classic of all the scenes of laughing gods brings us to the Titanic as an original form of the comic. The form of the Titans, it is true, has its prototypes in the Near East.²⁹⁷ Originally it belonged to strange gods of strange shapes, which appeared to the Greeks, from a certain distance, as having special, characteristic outlines. Hephaestus was in this way a god of a strange form, and so remained. Yet this is not the reason why he is laughed at. It was the Titanic itself which had been admitted to the Greek world of gods in the shape of Hephaestus. The other famous scene of laughing gods, the story of Aphrodite's adultery with Ares and the inventive cunning of the cuckolded Hephaestus,²⁹⁸ also brings us quite close to the Titanic element. It is Hephaestus who with his Promethean cunning and inventiveness catches the adulterers, puts his own shame on show, and thus makes himself all the more ridiculous. The impatient words of Poseidon ²⁹⁹ would make him feel how comically he was behaving, if the comic was not already part of his nature. But then there is the second hero of this story, the one who is laughed at—Ares. It is true to say that 'none of the other gods could for a moment be thought of in his position, not even Hermes who says that he would be glad to change places with him'.[300]   The two sons of Hera are worthy of one another.   Ares, with his insatiable love of battle, represents the very thing which in contrast to the divine could be called 'Titanic'.   And there is yet a third element, an aspect of what the Greeks themselves call 'the work of Aphrodite'.   The goddess herself is not comic.   The poet in fact leaves her entirely in the background, and 'by letting her person almost vanish shows the working of her eternal power'.[301]   In the aspect of her working which here comes to the fore the indecent and the comic are eternally combined, just as they are combined by the words of Hephaestus, who calls out 'ridiculous' and 'not allowed'.[302] A special mode of speech, for expressing the indecent and the comic, the 'Priapic', was similarly attributed to the Titans in the ancient world.[303]   It is not divine behaviour, but *in this sense* Titanic behaviour which arouses laughter among the gods.

Yet it must not be supposed that the poet forgot he was portraying his gods!   Nor can it be believed that he in some sense wished to destroy the gods whom he was portraying with such artistry.   The effect of the laughter of the gods is a different one.   The comic behaviour of Hephaestus in Book I of the Iliad, through which he betrays the Titanic strain in his nature, his uncouthness and crippled form, and thus provokes that loud laughter, is *intended* to provoke it.   In his good humour, characteristic like his innocent cruelty of a creature of the wild, he would like to relieve the tension between the great divine consorts, his parents Zeus and Hera—a tension in which the darker Titanic side of the characters of these two children of Cronos had shown itself.   Quarrelling and tension, fighting and bloodshed are in their nature Titanic.   Their Titanic *seriousness* is destroyed in this laughter.   That is the sense of it.   The laughter too, of course, wells up from an original Titanic source, from the very nature of the gods, as it was described certainly with greater freedom and probably also in agreement with mythological poems of the Near East, in an epic poem of pre-homeric character.[304]   In the Titanomachia of Eumelos or Arctinus, still composed in the style of the older epic, there was this verse: 'In the midst danced the father of men and gods'.[305]   The style of Homer, which is at the same time the Style of his religion, did not allow him to go so far.

The sense of the divine laughter and the essential unity of its two components—the laughter itself and the object of its relieving power, the Titanic—

becomes clear in the puzzling laughter of Zeus in Book XXI of the Iliad. The gods are fighting. The earth groans under them, the sky resounds. Zeus looks on—'and his heart laughs aloud for pleasure when he sees the gods meeting in battle'.[306] It is his Titan's heart which laughs, having woken in him memories of the old battle of the Titans. This is not a meaningless relic of an older poem, as it might be of the Titanomachia. The laughter of Zeus here has its reason and its meaning. Its reason is in the Titanic situation of fighting, but its meaning is that, once laughed at, the fighting of the gods loses its Titanic character. It may rather be called a blessed fight.[307] Gentle is the laughter of Zeus when Artemis, beaten by the smiling Hera, tearfully seeks refuge at his knee.[308] Even at an earlier time when, in Book V, divine blood was shed, the blood of the blessed goddess Aphrodite, Zeus's smile softened the pain and calmed the goddesses' strife.[309]

Like being and *noein*, so the Titanic element in the world of men and the laughter of the gods correspond to one another. Human Existence, being completely entangled in this element, and so far as it is not helped by Demeter and Dionysus or other sons of the gods like Asclepius, the Dioscuri, and Herakles, is miserable and from the divine point of view ridiculous, unimportant, in a way which cannot be further explained. But it becomes tragic, in its nothingness inexplicably important, in relation to the divine laughter. Zeus laughs aloud, the quarrel of indestructible forms becomes a divine comedy. Zeus let the gods quarrel but men moved him to pity.[310] The seriousness of the strife and tension, the fights and bloodshed of the unhappy sister-race of the gods attains, in comparison with the unseriousness of a 'blessed' fight, an enormous importance, and grows into a tragedy which demands divine spectators. In order to enhance the greatness and purity of the tragedy, Homer even allows nature to break its own laws. While Achilles is going into the battle in which gods will take part, his horses acquire human speech and strengthen the tragic certainty of his approaching end.[311] The battle of the gods is there only to increase the tragic importance of the battle of heroes. The effect of contrast here is not merely poetic or aesthetic, but an existential one.

The pure idea of the Greek religion even emphasises the illusion of the sacrificial cult—the self-deceit of men, as if they could deceive the gods! The sole illusion which it allows men in relation to the gods is the tragic importance of heroic existence as a spectacle for the gods. The most tragic thing about this importance is that it must after all disappear and turn to nothing before the laughter of the gods, when the eyes of the tragic hero are completely opened. For the divine laughter is not, as from the viewpoint of human misery it may seem to be, the laughter of an empty 'absolute blessedness', but it is the token of the complete all-embracing Existence which comprehends even the human and the Titanic.

DELPHI

and the cult of Delphic Apollo

86 *The Tholos of Delphi, seen from above*

87 *Delphi: view from the sacred site across the valley*

88 *The large temple at Delphi, dedicated to Apollo*

89 *View of the Stadium, the highest building of the site of Delphi, from the hillside*

90 *Part of the Sacred Way at Delphi with the treasure house of the Athenians*

91 *Aphrodite, Artemis and Apollo, from the east frieze of the Siphnian Treasure House at Delphi.*
Shortly before 525 B.C. Delphi Museum

92 *Statue of Apollo, from the west pediment of th*
Temple of Zeus at Olympia, finished in 456 B.C
Olympia Museum

93 *Scenes in the Palaestra. Vase painting by the Kleophrades painter, from Vulci, c. 500 B.C.*
Museum Antiker Kleinkunst, Munich

94 *Apollo crossing the sea on a winged tripod. Va.*
painting by the Berlin painter, 500–475 B.C
Vatican Museu

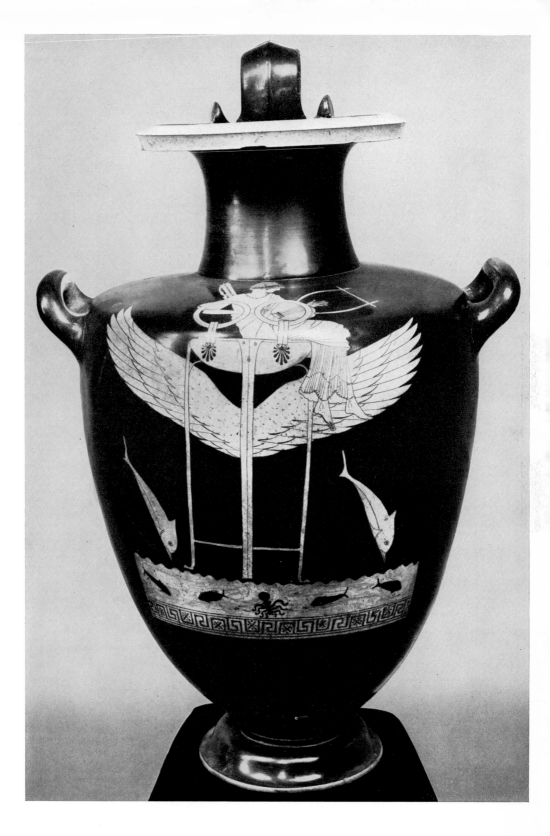

95 *Procession in honour of Apollo. Detail of the vase by the Kleophon painter, from Tomb 57c in the Valle Pega, Spina. 440–430 B.C. Archaeological Museum, Ferrara*

96 *Vase painting showing Apollo on throne at Delphi, omphalos and tripods at either side. (Reverse of the vase in plate 95)*

97 *Apollo, by the Peleus painter, from Tomb 617 in the Valle Trebba, Spina. Archaeological Museum, Ferrara*

98 *Apollo playing the lyre, accompanied by Hermes and Dionysus. A black-figured vase from Vulci. British Museum*

99 *Chariot race on the lid of the vase shown in plate 93; from Vulci. By the Kleophrades painter.*
Museum Antiker Kleinkunst, Munich

100 *Sacrifice before Apollo. Inside of a bowl by the Kalliope painter, 430–420 B.C. From Tomb 293 in the Valle Trebba, Spina. Archaeological Museum, Ferrara*

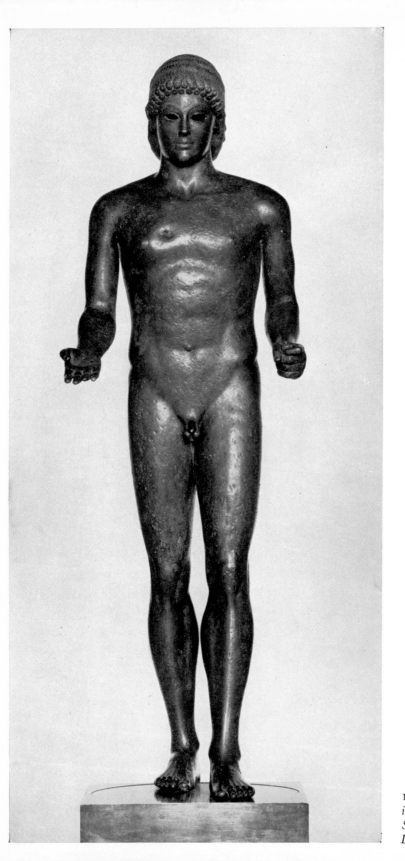

101 *Apollo of Piombino, found in the sea off Piombino, Etruria. Second quarter of 4th century B.C. Louvre, Paris*

CHAPTER VI

Man and God in the Roman View

I

THE LIFE OF THE FLAMEN DIALIS

WITH THE GREEKS IT IS THEIR POETRY WHICH provides a basis for characterising the form of the relation between god and man. Greek poetry contains actual accounts of the performance of the great Greek sacrifice in the Heroic Age. It even tells of the original, primordial performance of the sacrifice—in a narrative which may be classed with a whole series of similar myths in the archaic religions about the introduction of their sacred acts. In such primeval stories it is not the ordinary men of historical times nor—among the Greeks—the heroes who play the principal part, but primordial beings. The dominant beings of primeval times, who in their nature expressed the primordial character of the world, were identified by the Greeks with the uncouth forms of the Titans, whose name probably means 'kings'.[312] A whole world is conveyed by this name, a *primordial* world separate and remote from the new world of Zeus's sovereignty, yet at the same time a world made present and actual as the opposite of Zeus's world and therewith lifted altogether out of time. Just as raw, primitive Nature continues to exist even when the world is showing its spiritual face, so Zeus's sovereignty is completed by its opposite. As a background to it and to that of all the Olympian forms included in it there stands the sovereignty, defeated but still possible, of the Titans.

We see here the same polarity as in Heraclitus' pairs of opposites or as in Hesiod's statement that it is Night, with darkest Erebos, which gives birth to Day and brightest Ether, and continues to exist alongside them.[313] In the acts of the Greek cult, on the other hand, primordial things are always to some extent still present. They rise up not only in the worship of the great primordial goddesses but also when the Olympians are represented in the cult. The substance of the new gods is seen against this older background. It is, however, a pure substance, not mixed with temporal and corporeal matter, as it might be for instance with the form and colour of the sacrificial animals. For in early archaic times these must have played a big part. Such relationships, however, are completely archaic and by historic times had been pushed right into the background. The bulls sacrificed to Poseidon, for instance, were not only black, the colour which harmonised with the dark god, the husband of the earth-goddess Da, but also white and reddish.[314] The cult was still essentially representation, but it was always mythology, as interpreted in this later phase by poets and sculptors, which did the representing. In the Roman cult the picture is quite different. Here mythology and art seem to be lacking. Negative judgments like these, it is true, are always hazardous, in a field to which there is no immediate historical access—for the evidences date from periods which had already been subjected to the influence of classical Greek religion. But we may be all the more certain of what we know positively about the Roman case. For if we eliminate mythology and art, the only possible form of representation of the divine left to us is the cult itself. And in fact Roman religion does lay almost exclusive emphasis on the cult act, the ceremony, the life of the priests and priestesses. The corresponding phenomena of Greek religion do not bear comparison. They are far from being as characteristic of Greek religious Style as the instances known to us from Rome are of the Roman. For the principle which nearly all recent writers on Roman religion have taken as fundamental to their work is fully accounted for by the Roman Style. According to this principle, the religion of Rome is based exclusively on the exactly (*rite*) performed ceremonial act. Such performance fulfils and exhausts the *jus divinum*, or divine justice, the relation of the divine to men,[315] and correspondingly also the relation of men to the deity. Both for *pietas* and for *religio* Cicero gives this definition: *justitia adversum deos*, justice towards the gods.[316] In the sense of our detailed discussion of *pietas* and *religio*, we could say that the 'ritually' (*rite*) performed human act belongs to the 'sphere' of *pietas*. And this too belongs to the essence of *religio*, that no gap should be left, that nothing should be omitted, that no negative should show itself in respect of rightful action.

The cult act stands so characteristically in the centre of Roman religion that mythology, insofar as a Roman mythology existed at all, was completely overshadowed by it. Even art could play only a very small part there, and that only under Etruscan and Greek influence. We must, it is true, have a clear understanding of the meaning of a cult act. Many scholars believe that the strongly emphasised cult acts which are so characteristic of Roman religion can be explained only by an unattainable 'pre-deistic' period, in which there were no myths, a period before any worship of gods, and that they were originally acts of magic. But anyone who believes this must face the consequence that the historical religion of the Romans, who were so proud of their religiosity and so famed for it, was based on meaningless survivals from a primitive, exclusively magical period.[317] Before this, of course, the existence of such a primitive period must first be proved, and no such proof has ever been given. All we have, generally speaking, is a belief, in an assumption derived from a preconceived theory about the development of religions. In keeping with this assumption is a picture of Roman religion which sees only the formal side of what the Romans understood by the relation between man and god, that is to say 'just dealing',[318] and will hear nothing of any religious content in the Roman cult. Such a consequence is hard to accept in view of the evidences of history and the literary testimonies to the grandeur and purity of Roman *pietas* and *religio*. And it cannot be accepted at all when we know how little foundation there is for the assumption of a 'pre-deistic' period in Roman religious history.[319]

Religio in its fundamental meaning was a selecting and preserving activity. It contains the sound of the verb *religere*, even though the fathers of the Church preferred *religare*. One of the results of the selective activity of *religio* is undoubtedly to be seen in Rome's official attitude of reserve towards mythology, in the light of which the importance of the cult is brought out all the more strongly. This attitude corresponds to that same *epoche*—'restraint'—which we have shown to be the negative aspect of *religio*. It is also evident, however, that the attitude of reserve, when it functions as a selective activity, does contain something positive—what we may describe as an 'inner form'. It defines a Style which shows itself in all the phenomena of Roman Existence. At this point the question arises whether the Roman religion is not only not pre-mythological but actually post-mythological—retrospectively rid of its myths, 'demythologised'. This is a theory which must be taken seriously, and though in this extreme phrasing it too is mis-

M

taken, yet the myth-free atmosphere of the official Roman cult in comparison
with the abundance of myths in the surrounding world does testify to an
inner Form which chooses only the cult and rejects mythology.   When we
add that this anti-mythological tendency is paralleled by a similar feeling
against images of the gods,[320] it is clearly tempting to recognise in this Form
a more general type of religion which is found elsewhere in the history of
religions and not only at Rome.   A comparison could be made with the
Israelite religion, as we did in the case of the Roman religious consciousness.
For that reason the Roman Form must be scrutinised with special care,
independently of any theory and with reference only to the conditions in
which it originally arose.

The enquiry in which one set out to clarify the man-god relation as
understood by the Romans was in two stages.   In the first of these one
supposed [321] that the great number of names of gods and the multitude
of divine beings in ancient Roman religion was not due to some special
many-sidedness in their religious approach but only to their need of recognising the divine rule in everyday things, in what was near to them, and to
harmonise themselves with it.   Their limited view that all these gods existed
only for the Roman State, so it was argued, would have precluded the
possibility of their enquiring more deeply into the reasons for existence
and other questions of this kind.   There was no possibility of a Roman
saga about the origin of the world because the gods of the Roman State,
which would have had to be the bearers of such a myth, had only come
into existence with or after the creation of a Roman State.   Neither dogma
nor saga could have given any information about what existed before that.
If there were differences of age and rank among the gods, these could not
be determined by the time and manner of their appearance at the creation
of the world or in the history of the gods, but only by their having joined
the circle of Roman State deities at an earlier or later date, and by the extent
of their influence on the well-being of that State.   Personal qualities and
individual characteristics were supposed to have been lacking in these gods,
with their attachment to places and things.   They were simply ranged side
by side, without any other connection than that of neighbourhood and a
similarity in the manner of their influence.   Above all, according to this
view of Roman religion, divine marriages and divine genealogies were
unknown.   The accounts of such things given in later times were supposed

to be based entirely on poetic invention or on analogies drawn by scholars from Greek religion.

Such was, and today still is, the general view of Roman religion. A higher stage in the development of our knowledge, however, was reached when it was realised, in opposition to this view,[322] that there were on Roman soil definite traces of a mythology outside literature, untouched by the influence of Greek poetry. It was seen, too, that these traces were uniformly distributed among the ancient Roman, Etruscan, and Greek components of the historical Roman religion, and that the image of the divine as it appeared in them was not different from that which was expressed by the historical Roman cult. But a living intellectual exchange between myth and cult seemed no longer to exist in historical times. In its songs and formulae the cult was evidently concerned to avoid mythical things. It even passed over in silence those legendary ideas which seem so inseparable from the gods it had taken over from the Greeks. And in this behaviour we find a contrast between Roman religion and that of Italy. In the latter, tradition provides us with plenty of evidence for a lively interchange between cult and legend. From this set of facts it was inferred that the historical Roman cult—or the historical Roman religion (owing to the overriding importance of the cult the two were not kept distinct)—had been 'demythologised'. Historical evidence for such a process was found in Dionysius of Halicarnassus,[323] who describes the introduction of the cult of the Great Mother of Asia Minor, the *Magna Mater*, and makes a point of the manner in which the whole of the ceremonial determined by myth was discarded. On the other hand it was also a fact that the cult, though it made no reference to the myth in its formulae, yet did not dare to be inconsistent with it. The grouping of the pairs of gods at the *Lectisternia*, the Roman *Theoxenia*, showed that the order laid down by myth was being exactly followed.

Thus the theory of a mythless Roman religion, which represented only half the truth and gave rise to a false history of Roman religion, was followed in the scholarship of the twentieth century by that of a 'demythologised' religion. But this theory, too, could not be logically worked out, and it had to make one important concession. It had to allow that the myth was after all present in Roman religion, in its own way. For this theory the type of the 'demythologised' deity was the Roman Jupiter. Yet it is the figure of Jupiter which was perhaps the best demonstration of the presence of the myth and of the manner in which it found expression in the cult. It is in certain negative features of the Jupiter cult that a mythical prototype was so unmistakably outlined. We see from this example how the selective activity which is meant by *religio* in the strict sense was guided by the myth and how the myth conversely was translated into life by *religio*. A life which in fact originated in this way was central to the whole Jupiter cult. This, the life of the *Flamen Dialis*, was nothing else but a cult of Jupiter. When we come to consider this life we find ourselves at the very heart of the Roman religion. All the more important is it that our interpretation of this life should concern itself simply with the phenomena, and be content merely to describe them without seeking the help of analogies which would distract our attention from what is characteristically Roman. It should refrain also from introducing into the material handed down to us premature assumptions about the origin and nature of these phenomena.

One such premature assumption was the attempt to interpret everything we know about the *Flamen Dialis* as a survival of an ancient Roman priest-king.[324] Another was to explain all the *flamines*, holders of priestly offices attached to different Roman deities, in terms of an historical development for which there was no evidence. The sacred duties of the king, so it was supposed, had gradually been taken over by the *flamen Dialis*, the special priest of Jupiter, and the remaining duties had been transferred, after the abolition of the kingship, to the *rex sacrorum*.[325] Assumptions like these—apart from the origin of the office of *rex sacrorum*, as the obvious successor of the *rex*—are not supported by tradition and in fact explain nothing of what a *flamen*, and the *flamen Dialis* in particular, really was. Another view for which there is equally little foundation was that which understood the *flamen* himself as a thing, a sacred object,[326] a sort of fetish which had to be preserved with anxious care from any kind of harm or pollution. On the contrary, the *flamen*, especially the *flamen Dialis*, was identical with the life he lived. It was a life which was not his own but the realisation of a special manner of life. In this manner of life the wife of the *flamen Dialis*, the *flaminica*, also shared, with her children the *camilli* and *camillae*. It was a complete reversal of actual conditions in the ancient world to suppose that this manner of life was no more than an exemplary family life, the artificially realised ideal of a Roman family, and that its members worshipped Jupiter in a perfect way only because they had nothing else to do in a life given over to exemplary living.[327]   The position of the wife and children of the *flamen Dialis* did of course represent an essential aspect of his life.   But we do not need any special explanation of this aspect when we realise that the sole purpose of this life was to represent a mythological figure.

The lives of all three great *flamines*—the priests of Jupiter, Mars, and Quirinus designated by this name—had the character of a permanent festival.[328]   The *flamen* must not work, he must not even see other people at work.   Every day he keeps festival, and he bears the festival around with him.   Heralds run before him to order all work to stop within the range of his vision.   The *sacra*—the *caerimoniae*, or cult usages, which filled his life[329]— were defiled if he saw the unfestive work of hands.[330]   Festivity and cult in the life of the *flamen* were by no means confined to the times of sacrifice and the actual sacrifices which he offered to his god—Jupiter in the case of the Dialis—but his whole life must be considered festal, the performance of a cult.   A necessary part of this existence—this too is common to all three great *flamines*—was the ancient form of marriage by *confarreatio*.   Those chosen for it must be the offspring of marriages solemnised by this rite and must themselves be so married.   All these requirements, which applied not only to the *flamen Dialis*, served primarily to define a distinct, a festal manner of life, and the form of marriage was prescribed merely as a quite general condition for it.   It remains none the less remarkable that *confarreatio* itself belonged to the domain of Jupiter and that it was thus *his* priest, the Dialis, who at this ceremony performed the sacrifice together with the *pontifex maximus*.[331]   Moreover, the word *flaminica* without other additions always refers to the wife of the Dialis.[332]   He is the *flamen* whose wife plays her part beside him as a cult personage, sharing in the priestly dignity, while the wives of the Martialis and Quirinalis remain more in the background.

The life of the Dialis was more particularly characterised by its negative rules, which were exceptionally strict.   It is they which so sharply defined the festal manner of life which was characteristic of him *alone*.   Yet he is not called, for instance, *flamen Iovialis*, priest of Jupiter, but *Dialis*, priest of 'Day' or of 'Father Day', *Diespiter*.   *Dialis* is connected with *dies*.   It was the name given jokingly to one who was consul only for a day—*consul dialis*, 'consul of the day'.[333]   Varro gave the correct linguistic definition of *Diespiter*: *id est dies pater*.[334]   This name enshrines one aspect of Jupiter, while the name *Veiovis* stands for another aspect of the same god.   The different single aspects of the great god Jupiter were never completely split off, either in the case of Diespiter or in that of Veiovis. This latter too is spoken of in the literature as if obviously a 'Jupiter'.[335] The darker aspect of Jupiter indicated by the name *Veiovis* and translated by the Greek *Zeus Katachthonios*, the 'underworld Zeus',[336] is a much more sharply defined figure than that which among the Greeks was surrounded by the darkness of secret cults. *Veiovis* is much associated in Italy with the figure of Apollo,[337] always as the darker aspect of the Greek god. In Rome, however, his separation from the parent figure was never quite completed. *Veiovis* remained for the Romans *Ve-jovis*—no doubt different from Jupiter, whatever the syllable *ve-* may have meant,[338] and yet a sort of Jupiter. The unity of a Jupiter figure which was not only heavenly but also subterranean was never finally broken. We must still be aware of the darker aspect even when, as in the life of the *flamen Dialis*, only the bright side is spread out before us.

Everything in which death, an aspect of the 'chthonic' sphere, has part, was kept strictly away from this festal manner of life. The *flamen Dialis* must touch nothing dead nor walk in any place where there was a grave.[339] He must not look upon an army ready for battle. He must not mount a horse, whereas the *flamen Martialis*,[340] for instance, at the sacrifice of the October Horse, was concerned with horse and killing both at once.[341] This, and the circumstance that both he and the *flamen Quirinalis* were allowed to engage continually in warlike activities,[342] corresponds to the 'martial' character of their lives. The only thing permitted to the Dialis, on the other hand, was to take part in the Procession of the Dead, in which the ancestors were represented by their *imagines* or death-masks.[343] Thus there was no fear for his pollution when, for reasons which are not quite obvious, emphasis was being laid on the contact between the heavenly and the underworld spheres. There are various examples of this. Thus in the *fasti Praenestini*, or Praenestine Calendar, on 23 December there appears the festival of the dead called the *Larentalia*, with the gloss '*feriae Jovis*'; and in the *fasti Amiternini*, the Calendar of Amiternum, on 5 July, another grim celebration, the *Poplifugia*, carried the same gloss.

The dog and the bean were dear to the underworld beings, and were sacrificed to them. The *flamen Dialis* might not touch or even name either of them.[344] With equal strictness everything was forbidden him by which this sphere was known to the Greeks as belonging to Dionysus—an archaic

Dionysus who was a ruler of the underworld and a great hunter.[345] Uncooked meat was forbidden to the *flamen Dialis*, whereas in the cult of *Dionysus Omestes* raw meat was eaten.[346] Similar rules marked him off from the realm of Demeter, or Ceres among the Romans. The *flamen Dialis* was forbidden flour and yeast.[347] The realms themselves here matter much more than the Greek or Roman names of the deities in question. They probably had equivalent names in all the languages of ancient Italy. One animal and one plant of the Dionysiac domain were the goat and the ivy. Both were forbidden the Dialis no less than dog and bean.[348] Nor was an exception made of the highest plant representative of the Dionysiac domain, the plant in which the powers of the god were at their most exuberant.[349] For the Dialis was forbidden to go into a vineyard with overhanging vine-shoots.[350] On the other hand, he did have a part to play in the Lupercalia, at which a he-goat was sacrificed,[351] and it was he who introduced the vintage, by sacrificing a lamb to Jupiter and cutting the first bunch of grapes while the internal parts of the victim were being cut out. The vineyards around Rome stood under the dominion of Jupiter [352] at least from the time of the first ripe grapes in August. Perhaps this represented a limitation of the rule of an older and more savage wine-god.

Of the five positive duties of the *flamen Dialis* known to us [353] we have mentioned two. Two others were the sacrifice of the *ovis Idulis*, the white lamb, on the Ides of the month, and the sacrifice to *Fides*, both cult performances concerned with the brightest aspect of Jupiter. The fifth was his function at the *confarreatio*, the form of solemnisation of marriage which also had to precede his own birth. The confarreate marriage ranked among the Romans as the holiest form of union.[354] It was the only one in which the Dialis shared, both as priest who functioned at the ceremony and passively as the man who lived in a confarreate marriage. Otherwise the life of the Dialis was not permitted any form of union. He was not allowed to swear an oath,[355] to wear any knot in his clothing or headgear.[356] Even his ring had to be cut.[357] Anyone who entered his house in bonds had to be unbound and the fetters taken out again through the *impluvium*, the unroofed section of the *atrium*, or inner court.[358] His hair must not be cut by an unfree person.[359] Everything which grew upon him was subject to special treatment. The hair and nail clippings of the Dialis were buried under an *arbor felix*, a tree which did not belong to the underworld beings.[360] This was the positive counterpart to his being kept clear of every union. The essential thing in the life of the *flamen Dialis*, protected by so many negative rules, was thus shown to be free, unhampered growth.

Growth and freedom were both equally important in this pattern of life, and fastening is opposed to either. The domain of Veiovis represented the transition from the unfree sphere to that of freedom. In his sacred precinct lay the *Asylon*, through which slaves climbed out of the condition of slavery to the first stage of a free life.[361] Veiovis protected the Order of freedom at this lowest stage, with the rules and regulations of the client relationship.[362] Distinct from this was the next higher stage of freedom, represented by the life of the Dialis. This was manifested, as we have seen, in a complete freedom of growth. It was marked also by a special covering for the head. There is a striking analogy between the headgear by which the slave became a free man, the *pileus*, and that of the Dialis, the *apex*.[363] It shows that the life of the Dialis, though so far above the domain of Veiovis, was not entirely unconnected with it. The connection was that between two stages of growth. Growth here was considered not as historical progression but as a phenomenon which could take on different forms, stages of one another, in a process of free development. There was already development of a kind in the dark realm of Veiovis. Those set free were at the same time new-born, still at the childhood stage of growth and remaining there.[364] On the other hand the life of the Dialis, which was growth in full development, must have roots. Up in those radiant heights it must still have some connection with the dark underside of the world. It becomes clear what this was when we consider the one form of union permitted, and indeed essential, to the *flamen Dialis*.

The part played by the Dialis at the act of *confarreatio* may be assigned, undoubtedly, to the brightest aspect of Jupiter. The division of the Roman month, too, was connected with this aspect. It was divided in two parts by the day of the Ides, which itself was called 'Jupiter's surety,'[365] or 'Faith' (*fides*—in business, 'credit'). But Jupiter was also *Jupiter Farreus*,[366] the god through whom the spelt cake, the *far* of *confarreatio*, became divine and so expressed, by means of a sort of physical union, a spiritual union. It was this *real* union which emerged from the ceremony in full clarity and truth. The instrument of the physical act was a *thing*, and the more colourless and less specific a thing it was—like the piece of flint in the Fetiales, for instance, where it was the instrument of an international act—the more suitable it was for representing a spiritual reality, firm, clear and impersonal. Jupiter was there in the accomplishment of the rightful act, sure and hard as the stone. Was the act then accomplished by the stone? Yes, by *Jupiter Lapis*,[367] by 'Jupiter the Stone'! One ancient formula, with more exactness, uses the name Diespiter in this context.[368]

'If I knowingly betray this trust, may Diespiter sling me, without harm to city and citadel, out of all good, as I now sling this stone.' The marriage which comes about by *confarreatio*, a legal act before ten witnesses,[369] is a similar event. It is union—union however with another less clear and less sure kingdom in the world of men. It is a kingdom with which the Dialis is connected, through the *flaminica*, with whom he too shares a confarreate marriage. There is certainly good reason for the fact that she, the 'sacred wife of the Dialis',[370] can advise on favourable and unfavourable times for solemnising marriage.[371] Through her husband she is in relation with Jupiter, she is his priestess, *sacerdos Iovis*.[372] But she is also the one who as a woman has immediate knowledge, from her own experience, of that other darker and more dangerous realm. For the *flaminica* must be supposed to have had at least as close a relationship to Juno, the great goddess of that other realm, as every Roman woman had. According to our sources, indeed, the wife of the Dialis was related even more closely than that to the domain of Juno and so, through her, was the Dialis himself.

The flaminica was 'so to speak sacred to Juno'.[373] This is said in a context which makes it immediately intelligible why she was thought of as in the closest possible relationship to the goddess. She mourned as the twenty-seven rush dolls, called *Argei*, were thrown into the Tiber. The meaning of this performance is problematical. But the name *Argei*, 'those of Argos', indicates the favourites of *Iuno Argiva*, the inhabitants of Argos and in a wider sense the Greeks generally.[374] It is known that at the time when the *Argei* ceremony was introduced the Romans were conscious of a close relationship of the *flaminica* to the goddess who was then certainly identified with Hera. Tradition, which calls her only 'Dialis', is against her having been also the priestess of Juno. But her relationship to Juno was altogether natural. For the *flaminica* was a woman, and one united in matrimony with the *flamen Dialis* as Juno with Jupiter. As a woman she had part in something which the Romans called *Iuno*. The fundamental meaning of this word is the female counterpart of 'youth', a young female creature. As the Romans saw it, there was on the one hand the great goddess Juno, and on the other every woman possessed a young Female Nature, her special *Iuno*. This state of affairs may seem unclear at first but its peculiarity must be understood. For it will illuminate the relationship of the Dialis to the whole domain of Juno, which at first seems to have similar contradictions.

The great goddess Juno shows herself as the complementary half of Jupiter in the moving universe. To Jupiter belongs the bright time of the Ides, to Juno the dark time of the Kalends.[375] Just as on the one hand heavenly clarity and Jupiter, in his character as Diespiter, are inseparable for the Romans, so Juno on the other is inseparable from the dark time of new moon and the subterranean depths. The goat and the snake, which the *flamen Dialis* might not even name, are her dearest animals. At the cave of Lanuvium, where her domestic snake dwelt, the goat skin was part of her official clothing.[376] It is at least probable that, at a time and in a sphere where there could not yet be any question of an apparent 'demythologisation', there was a common worship of Juno Lucina and Jupiter.[377] Juno Lucina, the goddess of childbirth, in keeping with her nature lived in places where light and life come forth from dark depths. A point of time with this character was the day of the Kalends each month, which was presided over by Juno Lucina in common with Janus. A similar conjunction corresponded to Jupiter as Veiovis, as is attested by the dates of temple dedications.[378] Jupiter and Juno are like two hemispheres in their relation to one another. The brighter hemisphere reaches down into the dark depths, where it is in contact with the darker, and the darker receives just enough light from the brighter to raise it into the heavens.

The clear and firm relationship in which the great goddess Juno stands to Jupiter was reproduced by that between the *Iuno* of each individual woman and the *Genius* of every man. Everything which can be said of the Genius in the masculine domain was balanced by a corresponding feature of the Iuno in the feminine domain. Genius meant the 'begetter' by which a man was procreated and which continued his procreation. For that reason a man's birthday, on which his procreation first became manifest, was sacred to the Genius.[379] In the same way the birthdays of a woman were sacred to her Iuno *natalis*,[380] by the agency of which she entered upon a time to be filled with womanly life. Neither the Genius of man nor the

Iuno of women referred to any other life but the real earthly one. Roman women regarded their eyebrows as sacred to Juno.[381] There is a striking parallel to this notion in modern popular superstition and some rational ground for it has actually been supplied by recent medical observation. For there does appear to be a connection between the health and fertility of a woman's life and the growth of her eyebrows.[382] Corresponding to this attribution of the eyebrows to the domain of Juno was the fact that the male forehead was dedicated to the Genius.[383]

The divine element experienced in herself by every individual woman as her own Juno, her eternally self-renewing youthful femininity, was identified with one half of the world. It thus reached over into the universe itself and formed a hemisphere, complementary to the other hemisphere which on the cosmic scale was called 'Jupiter'. It remained, however, within the limits of a domain in which youth is the only determinant, the eternally fruitful youth of the world with the capacity for giving birth. Its counterpart in this same animal territory was the Genius as 'procreator'. In the Roman view the Genius with its relationship to the forehead reached out beyond this sphere. It soared into the domain of the high heavens, of Jupiter, even though it could not be said that 'the men had their "Jupiter" '. The Iunones of the women are at the same time the Juno of the world. On the male side there was nothing with a similar sort of name to correspond to this identity. Jupiter possessed his own Genius.[384] Between that which we can call the 'Genial' and that which we can call the 'Jovial'—to adopt a later linguistic usage—there was none the less a gap.

It is this gap which was filled, more or less, by the life of the Dialis. This life can be called, according to the later usage, 'Jovial', even when only those features of it are in evidence which correspond to the special epithet *dialis*. The confarreate marriage belongs to this life not only as a union, as a spiritual reality which must be preserved with exemplary faithfulness, but as a reality of life; not only as form but also as content. Not only was divorce forbidden the Dialis, but with the death of his wife he ceased to be *flamen*.[385] This has a matriarchal ring, as if it were a survival of a system in which the woman was the real holder of the priesthood.[386] Against this there is the fact that the *flaminica* could only be a *univira*—a remarried widow or a divorced wife were ineligible [387]—which would not usually have been the case with a matriarchal sovereign. What was required cannot be explained, only *described*—a whole consisting of two halves so applied to one another that they make a formally perfect pair. Strict rules ensured that this formal perfection, which corresponded rather to a mythological than to a formal idea, remained full of life. They have been handed down to us only in respect of the Dialis. In the case of one of them—the prohibition on long absence from Rome—it is known that the Dialis was at a disadvantage in his State life compared with the Martialis and the Quirinalis.[388]

They were rules affecting domestic life, as it were the nocturnal side of his 'genial' life. What we previously paraphrased as 'freedom and growth' coincides with the bright daytime side of his life. As the forehead is related to the head, so can the relation of the Genius to Jupiter be expressed in the Roman view. The impressive headgear of the Roman priests—not only the *flamines*, but also the *pontifices* and the *Salii*—the high cone-shaped *apex*, was pre-eminently characteristic of the Dialis. He was the only one who had to wear this uncomfortable hat *continually*. Not till the 1st century A.D. was he allowed to take off the *apex* at home.[389] And he *had to* take it off when he was preparing for death.[390] This forerunner of the Bishop's mitre seems to have been connected with the brightest 'jovial' sphere. The apex indeed gave distinction not only to the head but also to the forehead, which was sacred to the Genius. In the open air the Dialis was forbidden to take his shirt off, 'lest he should stand naked, so to speak, under the eye of Jupiter', thus it was expressly formulated,[391] and therewith once more the respect for the higher sphere was emphasised, whereas the Genius was related to the other, less bright sphere—as also was the life of the *flamen Dialis*, again regulated by strict rules.

His bed was as sacred as his hearth. Just as no one might bring fire out of his house for a sacred purpose,[392] so equally no one else might sleep in his bed.[393] Like the marriage bed of every Roman,[394] it was sacred to the Genius, but it had the additional peculiarity that its feet were painted with clay.[395] The intimate connection between this resting place and the earth was thus made obvious to the eye. A container with sacrificial cakes had to stand next to the bed,[396] an indication of ceremonies which made his repose into a cult act. Such an act was usually performed in honour of the Genius. At the wedding, for instance, it was the Genius in whose honour and with prayers to whom the marriage bed was prepared and from whom the bed had the name *lectus genialis*. The importance of the nocturnal side of the life of the Dialis was emphasised by the fact that though he might spend a day outside Rome, he must never spend a night outside it.[397] Later he was allowed two nights in which he might sleep in a bed other than his own, but never three successive nights.[398] The positive and negative rules together formed a meaningful whole. In this the nights of the Dialis were no less significant than his days. The fact that the nights of the man dedicated to Day were thus sanctified gave a clear outline to his mythological picture. It was simply the idea that the Heavens, usually so bright and clear, rested during the night in dark, procreative union on the earth.

Here we have a myth translated into human life. That was the meaning of all the prohibitions and ceremonies, which they declared and made intelligible. They made the myth as actual as it is humanly possible for it to be. In the life of his priest the Roman god of heaven walked among men. We have here a classical example of the truth that representation, or actualisation, is the essence of the cult. The view which denied all profundity to Roman religion because it had no myths about the origin of the world was evidently false. For here a comprehensive religious idea shone through as a myth continually realised in the life of the *flamen Dialis*. Something bright and exalted here turned its face to men and thus hinted also at a turning away from the darker spheres of existence—not in hatred but like a flower which turns away from its root, in growth and development. The roots reach down into those depths in which light and dark are united, giving rise to the living thing, so that what is free emerges from what is bound. There is nothing which conforms more exactly to the Roman idea of the State than this notion of cosmic brightness and clarity, the notion of a true Diespiter. Yet this notion cannot be detached from the more comprehensive one of Jupiter. It includes that which lies deepest, in which men directly participate and through which they have contact with the highest. As Jupiter in one of his aspects was Diespiter, so in another aspect he was *Jupiter Indiges*, the primordial procreative father, as this name must probably be interpreted.[399] The fact that Aeneas could be identified with *Iuppiter Indiges* is a sufficient proof of the existence of this aspect. To be primordial procreative father is divine, but it is also very human. The idea of a god who comprehends in himself procreative fatherhood and the highest spiritual clarity is necessarily both cosmic and merely

N

human. It is more or less realised in every spiritual man capable of father-hood.

Instead of a cosmogonic myth in words we have here a cult represen-tation, in which the origin and 'Jovial unfolding' of life, that is, the *content* of a cosmogonic myth, is not recited but actualised in the substance of a human life. In view of the wide dissemination of a mythical story of the separation of heaven and earth,[400] which of course presupposes their previous union, the question whether this form of representation was not in fact preceded by a myth in words must in all probability be answered in the affirmative. What we have here is a *Roman* form of representation, and at the same time a Roman form of the relation between man and god. It contains something more than a mere 'legal intercourse' although the Roman cult also includes the legalistic formalities of this relationship. The Dialis is 'so to speak a living holy statue'—so Plutarch formulates the relationship in this case.[401] Later accounts tended to the view of the *flamen* as a sacred object. We by contrast spoke of the life of the Dialis, but this view can be combined with that of Plutarch if we think of this 'life' as a 'substance', a substance composed of 'time' out of which is formed a living statue of Jupiter. This view is justified by ancient tradition. Nowhere is there a word about what the person of the Dialis may not suffer, only about what he must do or omit, so that his manner of life may be preserved from all disturbances. A sick Dialis was thinkable,[402] but a Dialis who deviated from the prescribed manner of life was unthinkable. The *temporal course* of his life was the cult act through which Jupiter was actualised. Further support for this view may be found in another case, which illustrates even more precisely the relation between man and god in such a form of representation.

A culminating point of the Roman cult of Jupiter was an act in which the god, in his capacity as conqueror, was represented by a man, the trium-phant general. Originally the *triumphus*, to judge from his name, which comes from the Greek *thriambos*, a Dionysiac celebration, was probably not associated with that idea of Jupiter *Optimus Maximus* which is characteristic of the historic Roman religion. None the less, the god in triumph was here represented by a piece of human life, a duration of time raised to high tension by the festival spirit. The view was not that Jupiter had brought about and effected the victory, but that he was himself the victor. The triumph was not held in his honour but it was he himself who triumphed. That is why the triumphant general drove around in the insignia of the god.[403] This corresponded to the Roman concept of godhead, insofar as a god for the Romans was always an agent.[404] Just for that reason he could not have that concreteness and abundance which we admire in the Greek gods. For the Romans the godhead expresses itself not in Form, but in a temporal sequence of decisive acts. One such act was the victory to which a cult act, the Triumph, corresponded. The general performed this act as Jupiter, just as in the act of victory he had not really been himself but Jupiter. And that was what he was in the Triumph, but only in one single act, during a procession to the Capitol, until the moment when he laid down his bay wreath before the god.[405]

The *flamen Dialis*, on the other hand, did not merely perform one act of Jupiter, but entered into a whole aspect of the god. In this case we see that the Roman concept of godhead was reduced to that of an agent not in the historical Roman religion but later on, in the Roman theology of Varro's time, in the first century B.C. The Roman gods appear as abstract and without abundance only when we think of time as empty and not filled with the stuff of life. The Dialis with his life entered into an aspect of divinity which in its form was an idea but in its content appeared in time, formed so to speak from the stuff of life. It had kinship with human life and could be represented by human life. But it stood also above it. For so long as human life existed, it would always be able to represent it. Such an aspect had its own kind of concreteness, empirical rather than intelligible. It was experienced, lived: in a passive, devout fashion when one followed it involuntarily and could not do otherwise; in an active fashion when one by choice—in Roman terms 'religiously'—entered into an aspect of the world evolving in time. That is what the *flamen Dialis* did as an example to everyone.

2

RETROSPECT

At the beginning of this chapter we started out by comparing the Greek and the Roman religion. We showed that the religion of the Greeks might with more justice be called a 'mythological religion' than that of the Romans. For classical scholarship both of them were—in contrast to the doctrinal religions—cult religions. This description, however, must remain an empty one so long as we only consider what kinds of religious content they excluded and not what they actually contained. We may, if we choose, call the positive content of the ancient religion 'cult'. But we must realise that this word signifies a relationship which is in its essence actualisation—the representation of something real, something which is never simple, but manifold and various, as manifold and various as the aspects of the world in fact are to men. This real thing has the capacity to become actual in a festive way, that is to say even more present than are the most present things of everyday. To this *higher form of reality*, which belongs only to the festal world, there correspond those special forms of representation which can in the widest sense be called 'cult'. Besides the cult in the narrowest sense they include also poetic and artistic representation. In this sense mythology too would be 'cult' if it were not, above all, word, statement, speech, with its own movement and development, knowing no bounds. The cult on the other hand is sharply bounded. Within its bounds it consists of actions which run their course in time but also of pictorial elements with which it approaches the timeless. Our comparison of the Greek and Roman religion attributed the more pictorial cult to the Greeks, while we saw the Roman cult as one which exhausted its possibilities in action. In *this* sense, of the two ancient religions, the Roman could be called pre-eminently the religion of cult.

The fact that it was so for so long—throughout Roman history as known to us—we attributed to the efficacy of *religio*, of careful 'choice'. This selective activity of *religio* used to be all too readily interpreted as mere traditionalism, based on a primitive, 'pre-deistic' state of Roman religion. The existence of any such state in Roman religious history remains, however, an unproved hypothesis. There was an opposing view which had to be treated with more respect. It may perhaps have been possible that the Roman cult represented not a pre-mythological past but a 'demythologised' one. This view merits special consideration in view of the picture we today have of the Mediterranean world. For reasons of historical insight, moreover, we were bound to give preference to the view that it was not a barren conservatism which was realised in *religio* but a living inner form—the

Roman form. The theory of 'demythologisation' is based on a painstaking interpretation of the tradition. It positively demanded a view of *religio* which accorded it more than a mere power of conservation.

Just as the aptitude of the Greeks for *theoria* helped them to create clear images of the divine, so the Romans were enabled by their *religio* to realise the divine deliberately in life and action. An example of such *deliberate realisation*, which was as much exalted above the ordinary life of man as a Greek Zeus-image was above the bodily appearance of Zeus-like men, was the life of the *flamen Dialis*. This life was just as much an actualisation of the divine as the famous work of Pheidias or its predecessors, Homer's descriptions of the father of gods and men. It was, however, an actualisation in Roman Style. An activity of *religio* which makes divine images out of the stuff of life, as the Greek sculptors made them from marble, goes beyond anything which could be implied by a negative word like 'demythologisation'. This is a very one-sided, and therefore false, term for anything as positive and creative as the activities of priestly Romans in working out a relationship between the archetypal world of mythology and the ectypal world of life and history—to use the terms I introduced in the first chapter of this book. This relation between myth and life—*mythos* and *bios*, the myth as prototype, the life as imitation—is itself archetypal. It was never more than approximately realised, and there were many forms of realisation, various in style. The purest form was that defined by Malinowski in the light of his experience—'the statement of an original, greater and more important reality by which the present life, destiny, and activity of men is determined'—'something which happened once upon a time'.

The Romans had remained even closer to this conception than the Greeks. The Greek stories about the gods take place, it is true, in primeval times, but they are presented under a timeless aspect—as though in a special part of space in which, in contrast to the world of men, time does not exist. Whatever men do, it is not regarded either as the continuation of the stories about the gods nor as their repetition. It was otherwise with the Romans. For them, any remnant of a great earlier myth which was not already embodied in a cult life, as in the life of the *flamen Dialis* (and doubtless the life of the Vestal Virgins was also of this kind), constituted the history of the Italian primeval age. It only became 'cosmic' when the Romans made it so by turning it into their own great history. They were consciously repeating themselves. Vergil's Aeneid is an expression of the Roman concern to realise the myth. His poetic effort operates within Roman religion just as faithfully as Dante's within his Catholic religion. The Roman attitude to myth shows itself, apart from the cult, in the fact that for them the past was continually effective in the present. There was no frontier of time between myth and history, both were lines which met one another in the uniform flow of time. 'Thus myth became *historia sacra*, of normalising importance for the present.'[406]

Thus myth in ancient religion has two forms corresponding to the two classical cultures of the Mediterranean world. The Greeks developed it in images which require the greatest openness of mind and are *intelligible* to such openness. With the Romans the myth appears more conceptual, abstract, schematic,[407] but it demands a special kind of openness of mind for everything which belongs to time, and above all for one's own life with which one directly *experiences* time. They are two aspects which mutually complete one another, since they are aspects of one and the same world, the world which in its festive quality was actual for the people of antiquity and could become even more so. Both aspects united make the world of the religious Greek or Roman accessible to us, so far as this is still possible. This access can only be attempted through ideas, which we may consider as the fundamental ideas of ancient religion.

These fundamental ideas derive, so far as their form is concerned, from the Greek and Roman Existence. In their content they are primordial experiences of man expressed in myths. The observations which I have here set down dealt with them from the viewpoint of the stylistic Form in which they appeared to the Greeks and Romans. The two people were at the same time characterised by this Form. The character portrait thus obtained consists, it is true, only of outlines. It is more geometrical than pictorial. Nor can it be argued that this outline drawing is as valid for the pre-Homeric and old Italian period, or for the late period, as it is for the post-Homeric and in Rome for the historical period of religion. All that can be said is that a study of these *Forms*—even for those who take a different view of their *content*—does bring us closer to a picture, which can never be completely accessible, of the two ancient religions and ancient civilisation as a whole.

ROME

and the Roman cults

102 *Marble statue of Augustus as a*
priest, c. A.D. 20, from the
Via Labicana, Rome.
Museo Nazionale, Rome

103 *'Sacrarium' from the Casa del Cenacolo, Pompeii*

104 *Shrine of the Lares in the house of the Vettii, Pompeii. Third quarter of 1st century A.D.*

105 *Altar with festoons and bucrania. Archaeological Museum, Naples*

106 *Altar of Caius Manlius showing a scene of sacrifice, perhaps to the Genius Imperiale. Period of Augustus. Lateran Museum*

107 *Altar dedicated to the Lares of Augustus, from the Vicus Sandaliarius. A.D. 2. Uffizi, Florence*

108 *Frieze from an altar which stood in front of the Temple of Neptune, Rome. Erected by Cn. Domitius Ahenobarbus, found near the Palazzo Santacroce. c. 40 B.C. Louvre, Paris*

109 *A frieze representing the Sulcus primigenius. Middle 1st century A.D. Aquileia Museum*

110–111 *Relief representing Vicomagistri, the presidents of the Vici, whose duties included in imperial times the upkeep of the cult of the Lares compitales, the Lares Augusti and the genius of the emperor; c. A.D. 40. Vatican Museum*

I *Triumphal Arch* II *The birth-sign of Augustus* III *Temple of Mars Ultor*

IV *Arches for the dead at Actium* V *Apollo Palatinus* VI *Curia Julia*

VII *Triumphal chariot* VIII *Victoria in the Curia* IX *Laurel trees*

112 AUGUSTAN COINS

113 *Scenes from the haruspicatio on the Capitol (detail). Second decade of 2nd century A.D. Louvre, Paris*

114 *Suovetaurilia carried out by an Emperor; from the Palazzo San Marco, Rome; Flavian period. Louvre, Paris*

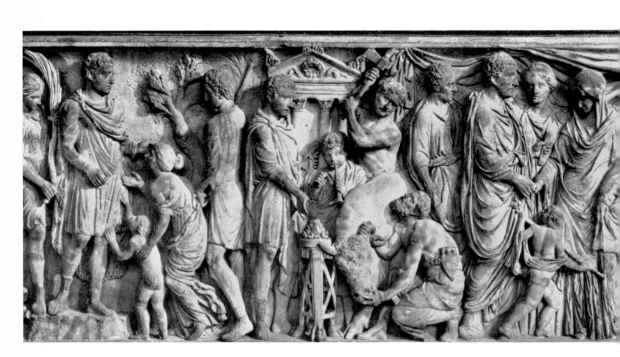

115 *Sarcophagus showing the life of a Roman citizen; Flavian period. Uffizi, Florence*

116 *Sacrifice. Part of the Ara Pietatis of Claudius. Villa Medici, Rome*

117 *A relief showing a procession, from the Ara Pacis, Rome; 13–9 B.C.*

118 *A relief with priests and the Imperial Family, from the Ara Pacis, Rome; 13–9 B.C.*

119 *Roman Haruspex, taking the haruspicatio on the Capitol, second decade of 2nd century A.D*
This and Pl. 113 are details from the same frieze

120 *Trajan pouring a libation on an altar. Trajan's column, Rome*

121 *Banquet of the Vestals, a fragment from the Ara Pietatis; c. 1st century A.D.
Museo dei Conservatori, Rome*

122 *Pompa before Ludi of a Sevir, from a tomb at Amiternum. 1st century A.D.
Museo Nazionale, Rome*

123 *Septimius Severus and his wife Giulia offering a sacrifice, from the Arch of Septimius Severus, Rome*

124 *A Vota Suscepta before crossing the Danube, Trajan's Column, Rome*

Epilogue

THE RELIGIOUS IDEA OF
NON-EXISTENCE

I

ONE HUMAN EXPERIENCE from which attempts have been made to derive not merely ancient religion but all religion is death. We have been offered statements like this: 'All faith is faith in another world, the fate of the soul after death constitutes in all religions the centre of religious thought.'[408] No doubt this is an extreme generalisation. Yet here, at the end of a book which has sought to understand the ancient religions as 'religions of the certainty of the universe', certainty, that is, of the non-human foundations of the world of men, we must give some consideration to the question how the 'other world' is regarded in these and similar religions of 'this world'. We have spoken of the fundamental outlines of the ancient religion without having said a word about Greek and Roman notions of the soul. There is need of a new, exhaustive treatment of this subject,[409] and we shall be making only a small, though indispensable, step towards it if we now deal with the question here.

Death was taken very seriously by the ancient Greeks and Romans. It was not doubted that man is subject to death as to a ruler over existence. It would be easy to say that religious man in antiquity was always preoccupied with the problem of death and that it was his religion, with its ideas about death, which first gave him answers to it. In reality the ideas of the most ancient Greek philosophers have not been transmitted to us in such a form that we can say what *questions* they asked and how they asked them. The art of asking questions was a much later achievement of ancient philosophy than that of *viewing* and *stating* what was important in the world. Philosophic ideas existed before philosophic questions were asked. Ideas do not presuppose the asking of questions, especially not child-like questions. There is no justification for assuming that such questions were in fact asked by serious thinkers of antiquity. Questions are first formulated for the benefit of ignorant people and schoolchildren after knowledge and vision have already been consolidated. Or they emerge when the solid foundations begin to dissolve.

Least of all do religious ideas exist in order to answer questions. Religions are not solutions of primeval problems. Rather they add considerably to the number of problems. The religious ideas and the mythological accounts of them themselves become assumptions on which questions and answers are based. Even when a god has appeared to a man, he can put questions about that appearance. All the more will questions be put as the end of a religion is approached. In the end the gods and all religious ideas become 'questionable'. In their original, living, valid form religious ideas belong to a quite different sphere from the asking of questions and posing of problems or from the giving of answers and solutions. They do, however, show a certain similarity with the oldest philosophic ideas in that they do, like them, contain an attitude of man to the world. The reality of the world manifests itself in them in one of the forms which the world itself offers. It shows itself to man, who as knower and perceiver confronts both form and content and holds firm what is offered him, as one aspect of the world, a sort of idea of the world.

We have learnt to know this attitude of ancient religious man as the attitude of *aidos* and *sebas* or else as the attitude of observance, of regulating one's life according to rule, of *religio*. In its highest form, the Greek, it is in contact with the attitude of the philosopher. However, the *noein* of the philosopher is directed at a special transparency of the world, at penetrating to naked being. This was particularly the case in archaic Greek philosophy. Plato and Aristotle did at least give pride of place to 'wonder' as the origin of philosophy.[410] *Thaumazein*, *thauma*, and *thambos* are connected with *sebas*, but on the evidence of the Greek language they had no religious consequences.[411] Yet not even *thauma* originally meant what was there to provoke questions and make a starting point for philosophising, but only that which it was worth while to view.[412] The archaic philosopher was not the man of *thaumazein* in this sense, but nor was he in the later, Socratic sense. Without putting questions he was convinced of the necessity of holding fast to the one essential thing in the world, its meaning and its truth, the *logos* and the *aletheia*. And all he did was to proclaim this essential thing as the man who looks out over the many particular aspects of the world and thinks about them, about the gods. He was the man, as we have put it, of ultimate penetration.

The ideas of ancient religion about death are not answers to questions. They express the attitude of ancient man to the reality of death and are founded in the idea of death itself, on the knowledge of death, and they particularise that knowledge. Men are mortal. This is how the most general and the simplest knowledge of death has always had to be formulated. Yet this knowledge, insofar as it represents a *religious idea*, is not the mere result of an inference which can be reached by thinking and which is formulated purely as thought. It is a knowledge which wakes a peculiar 'echo' in us, even when it proceeds from experiences of human society. It is only through this echo, through our knowledge of the fact that this simplest and most general knowledge of death concerns *us too*, that its effect on us is so convincing. It becomes like the other world realities, a festal idea—as the idea of death always is.[413] Only this echo is for us the token that death belongs to the realities at all.

It cannot be denied. If there is any reality in the world then death is one, a mighty, spiritual reality which leaves no one 'cold'. It is not like any other subject of knowledge, but touches everyone with dread. If the study of religion attempted to ignore this fact and to treat the idea of death only as a logical inference and not as a psychic reality, it could rightly be accused of unreality, of detaching itself from all actuality, and therewith also of being unscientific. What is real in the case is the death of an individual, the very one who has the idea about death. It is this which seems to provide a clear and firm foundation for ideas of death in general. The difficulties for the view of ancient religion taken by this book seem to begin when we look for the objective content of these ideas. For it is not the world which seems to be expressed in them but thoughts which go much further than that, having to do with a world beyond this one and lying far outside it. Ideas about death seem to represent an exclusive, one-sided affair of the soul, so that there is *nothing* corresponding to them in the world, unless it be in some supernatural order of things.

This is how it *seems*. For the simplest knowledge of death which is at the same time a psychic reality for us, because it also includes our own death, can probably be taken as a *firm* foundation for all religious ideas of death. It cannot, however, be maintained that it is a *clear* idea for the religious man or for the science of religion. There is one reproach which can be levelled at all earlier research into notions about the soul and the world beyond. It has neglected the important distinction between a man's own death and that of *another*. The first to make this distinction were Rilke and recent philosophers. If I quote them in what follows, it is not in adherence to any particular school of philosophy but simply to make use of their clear-cut formulations in order to throw light on a universal human topic.

2

Even if we wanted to choose, as the starting point for an investigation of the religious idea of death, experiences of the soul which belong in the domain of parapsychology, we should still have to start from the reality of death and its given content of ideas, with their apparent contradictions. We have to say with Max Scheler, 'The first condition for a life after death is death itself.' It was this philosopher who remarked, no doubt rightly, that the chief reason why modern man is not much interested in a life after death is that, essentially, he denies death.[414] The definitions of death given by natural science are in fact uncertain.[415] The medical view is that the departure of life can be delayed *ad infinitum*. That is why Scheler begins his examination of the after-life by elaborating a theory of the knowledge of death. This is probably the only correct scientific procedure. It was expressed by Heidegger perhaps even more sharply: 'We cannot even ask at all, with sense or reason, what is *after death*, until we have understood death in its complete ontological essence.'[416] This methodological principle and the axiom of the priority of death over the after-life is just as valid when our subject of consideration is not the life after death in general, but the ideas of ancient religion about death and the after-life.

Religious knowledge is far ahead of philosophic knowledge in directness. Heidegger correctly recognised that the problem presenting itself for his 'existential' analysis could be most directly illuminated from a primary source—the views of death among 'primitives' and their actual behaviour towards death in cult and magic.[417] One of the most genuinely prehistoric views of death, that which we find in the labyrinth image, to give only one example, shows how much richer, more complex, and meaningful a mythological idea can be than an ancient philosophical one.[418]

The ancient philosopher conceives death as a 'polar' opposite of life, connected with it in such a way that the one can only be present in the absence of the other. For Heraclitus this form of connection was equivalent to a deeper identity—let the name of the 'bow' (*biós* equated with *bíos*) be 'life', but let its work be 'death'. Or to take an example from the archaic Greek religion, let Dionysus and Hades be the same.[419] In Plato's *Phaedo* this opposition is the guarantee that death can do nothing to the soul. The one excludes the other, understanding *psyche* in the sense of 'soul' and 'life.'[420] Epicurus takes his stand on this exclusiveness of life when he says: 'When we are present, death is not present, and when death is present we are not.'[421] On the other hand, mythological narratives of the origin of death are everywhere found as part of the myth of the origin of the normal life of humanity.[422] Death is neither identical with life nor does it exclude it, but it belongs to it as an essential component—a component of the infinite lifeline of the tribe, which is continued by every death, in the succession life-death-life. This idea of the relatedness of life and death as a beginning and a setting, followed in succession by a new beginning, could be derived from the heavenly bodies, especially the moon, or from plant growth and the generation of animals. It is experienced in divine Forms which die and are yet eternal, especially in moon-like goddesses.

3

The idea here indicated of 'life-death-life' stands over the difference between 'one's own' and 'another's death', but does not exclude this or the mythological ideas based on it. Above all it does not exclude the idea of the Hades frontier. The determination that death has occurred is on the one hand a practical matter—today a medico-legal one. Theoretical science with its definitions, as we have seen, is uncertain on this point. On the other hand the determination of death is also a religious and mythological matter. With the consciousness that death has occurred, truth in the form of myth springs up in the soul of the survivor. This truth is now the frontier which finally divides the dead from the living, no matter how near or how far the place where they are laid to rest or thought to be.[423] The one thing about the realm of the dead which is today still unshakably real is its frontier. It has a psychic reality, but not *only* a psychic one. It becomes noticeable, beyond all dispute, when someone dies. Attic grave urns (lekythoi) show the dead as in life, at home with their relations and friends, receiving them, adorning themselves. But in the same picture the grave too is visible, and Hermes or Charon in an Acherontian landscape.[424] For the one who crosses the frontier the realm of the dead has sprung up in his life, at home. For the survivors the frontier is there, invisible.

What does it consist of, this psychic reality? What is this inconceivable something, so hard to determine scientifically and yet fatally real, for which the only appropriate determination is the mythological 'frontier of Hades'? The dead body and the transformation of a living man into a corpse belong to the world and not to the soul. The 'death of another' is not an internal concern of man except insofar as it awakens that peculiar 'echo'. However real the Hades frontier may be for a living man, what he experiences in it is only the 'death of another'. His 'own death' is yet more real for him, it is the really real thing from which the other death, the death of another, gets its psychic reality. There is a difference between the two deaths which is directly experienced by all of us, even when it is not even admitted by us and for that reason not clearly imagined. This difference has been given a precise philosophical formulation: 'We do not in any real sense experience the death of others but are at most "present" at it.'[425] What is real and primary is the psychic reality conveyed to us by that echo. To quote the philosopher further, 'Death, if it "is" at all, is essentially my death.'[426] Only as 'one's own death' does death have any psychic reality.

But is the idea of 'one's own death' conceivable at all from its subjective, spiritual side? From the objective side, of course it is conceivable. Objectively, the world contains, first as a possibility, then as its fulfilment, our own death, just as it contains in the past all completed death and all the dead.[427] But how is it with our own *perishable nature?* Is it at all possible for us to have a *direct* attitude to it? Can we directly experience 'our own death' in our own life, or read it in the book of the world, as we read there the idea of the inter-connectedness of life and death?

The saying of Epicurus argues against it. 'Death is no concern of ours. For when we are present, death is not present, and when death is present, we are not.' And yet it was Epicurus in particular for whom death in an important fashion was always present. His thorough treatment of the subject was criticised in this sense by his ancient opponents.[428] But it is not until much later times that we find a special *sense* of 'one's own death'. Rilke was the first who spoke of it as the 'great death', the death 'which everyone has in him', 'of which we are nothing but the husk and the leaf'. For, he said, 'this is the fruit on which everything depends'.[429] But we must first acquaint ourselves with the bare facts as they are experienced by modern man. We shall find Scheler's 'theory of the knowledge of death' in some measure suitable for this purpose. We shall not use his system of thought to *prove* that 'our own death' is for us the primary one. His genuine experience is shared as *living* experience by every one of us, however paradoxical that may sound. But we may succeed in making this experience intelligible, rather as we did with the experience of the festival, and in endowing it with some needed clarity.

A man, even if he were the only living thing on earth, in some sort of way would know that death was going to overtake him—so runs Scheler's train of thought.[430] The certainty of this is involved in every phase of life, however small, and in the structure of his experience. The 'idea and nature of death' is one of the constituent elements of all vital consciousness. We experience and see in every indivisible moment of our life process something 'passing' and something 'coming'. In every present moment we are affected by the feeling that something in general is 'passing away' and that something else in general is 'to be expected', independently of what it may contain. The total extent of what is 'passing' and what is 'to come', with the advance of the life process, is always being distributed afresh in a characteristic direction. That which is passing increases, while that which is to come decreases. The extent of what is present existence gets more and more strongly 'compressed' between these two. For the child the present is a broad, bright surface of the most colourful existence. This surface decreases in extent with every advance of the life process. It becomes smaller and smaller, more and more compressed. For the young person the future is there like a broad, bright corridor stretching out into the invisible distance. But with every piece of life that is lived there is per-

ceptibly less room for life still to be lived. The livable life is steadily con-
sumed while life already lived increases. This is the 'direction of death'.
We experience it, in the natural structure of every living moment, as a
sense of an increasing difference between two lengths. The future shrinks
as the past grows longer. Death is not just an empirical constituent of our
experience, but it is of the nature of every life experience, our own among
them, that it has the direction of death. Death belongs to the form and
structure, internal and external, of every life as it is given, our own among
the rest. It is not a frame which has by chance been added to the picture
of particular psychic and physiological processes, but a frame that is itself
part of the picture. Without it the picture would not be a picture of life.

The modern philosopher speaks to us men of today in our own language.
He remains in the realm of the subjective, and at that is not even exhaustive.
In every life he ignores its spiritual content, which for an individual who sees
life hurrying away from him with advancing age may well be of most
value.[431] By contrast with this philosopher we may turn to a man much
richer in the experience of life—Berdyaev, who says, 'Suffering passes, the
having suffered never passes. . . . Victory may indeed be achieved over what
has been experienced, and yet that experience is still in our possession as a
permanent enhancement and extension of the reality of our spiritual life.
What has once been lived through cannot possibly be effaced. That which
has been continues to exist in a transfigured form. Man is by no means a
completely finished product. Rather he moulds and creates himself in and
through his experience of life.'[432] Yet insofar as man is a living being, the
structure of his life corresponds exactly to that idea of the interconnection
of life and death in which this important, natural component of life is to be
found. What Goethe would call the entelechy, or full development, of the
spiritual form of an individual may give promise of something more than
one single, unique life, yet everyone in his life must experience 'his own
death'. Once he has attained a state of spiritual fulfilment, he may perhaps
contemplate the world with the openness of mind of the ancients, culminating in their *theoria* or *religio*. Yet there too he cannot fail to read the message
that human existence is in its nature transitory.

Scheler describes the death-direction from the point of view of a man
turned in on himself. For the ancients the corresponding description,
although it also included a man's *own* death, would have to be a description

not of his inner life, but of the world of men. This is the world which contracts around us in our experience of the death-direction, indeed independently of our actual experience, and which in its relation to ourselves approaches closer and closer to rejection and complete negation. In our experience of our own death a real aspect of the world reveals itself to us, announcing non-existence, the total absence of room for life. It is not easy to formulate the idea of non-existence philosophically and the task of doing so was left for relatively late times. But in the study of religions this philosophically 'difficult' idea of non-existence is the very one which can serve as a model to show how an ancient religious idea is constructed, for it is one which is at the heart of many mythological tales, incorporated in images of the gods and descriptions of another world.

4

We say the religious idea of non-existence. Could we not just as well talk of the 'myth of non-existence', a myth worked into particular mythical tales, incorporated in images of the gods and descriptions of another world? It can be done. The choice of the word 'idea' instead of 'myth', however, gives more prominence to the visual appearance, while 'myth' emphasises the content of what is stated or appears as a picture.[433] When the dying Greek invokes 'the gates of Hades',[434] this is a *picture*, but not only a picture. It is also the viewing and naming of a reality. In particular, since an 'after life' in Hades is not necessarily implied by it nor self-evident in it, the reality viewed is that of non-existence. It is real because the impending non-existence of the speaker is an actual part of the world. It will be that he will not be! Nor is the god Hades himself only an image. He too is an 'actual' god. Because of him and in company with him the other death deities of the ancient world, which do not guarantee an 'after life' but only the reality of death, we are forced to recognise that the ancient religious view, in its unreflective fashion, includes non-existence among the forms of existence, that it extends the all-embracing realm of being to non-being itself.[435] It is rare for an ancient 'religious idea' to be found in such exemplary form as here, where its content—non-existence—although really there for us all in the world, is conceivable *only* as an idea and *only* in pictorial form, by the one who experiences and knows it, and only by him.

There is a big series of Roman tomb inscriptions which describe the reality of death as a world of negation and privation—a world of evil, of darkness, of stillness, of cold, of ugliness. A survey made in the spirit of these interpretations[436] yielded the following statement: 'The mythical view clothes even non-existence with a shape and gives a form to nothingness. The Greek and Roman belief in immortality is almost always treated by historians of religion as if we here had to do with ideas about an actual afterlife in the grave or in the underworld—a mistake which more than anything else shows up the immense gulf dividing the ancient from the modern view. For these ideas are far removed from a belief in immortality. On the contrary, they are direct forms of expression of the human condition in death.' The apotheosis of the dead which we encounter in archaic and then in later imperialistic times was something quite different. This too was a highly contradictory idea. Generally speaking, the state of death is described in the tomb inscriptions as something objective. It appears as a paraphrase for 'objective non-existence', the thing we are headed for as we move in the direction of death.

These paraphrases have nothing to do with a capacity or incapacity for abstraction. The withdrawal of itself which life in fact performs was expressed by analogy, in terms of existence. It is quite in the spirit of Greece and of antiquity when Plato says, 'Non-Existence in some sense exists.'[437] The language of the unreflected experience of life puts for 'non-existence'—'death'. Yet death too has its place assigned to it in the Greek conception of the universe. Death and its domain are bounded. The world which contains *our* non-existence therein displays one of its aspects, whether a monstrous, beast-like, or man-like, or even a motherly face, or only emptiness and cold and gloom—an aspect at any rate which we know and recognise. We know it from inside as a capacity of the world to undergo a transformation which for us is final. The dread of this change springs from the negation and privation which it means for us. And what makes it all the more dreadful is that it does not face us with the possibility that the existence of the world itself could be shattered, but only with our own reduction to nothingness. For in this aspect of the world there is displayed to everyone his own death. The death-aspect of the world is, in a primary and immediate fashion, identical with the experience that the whole universe stands before us, but with diminishing room for ourselves. Some room in another world is not excluded by this knowledge, yet it must be more appropriate to the state of death than to that of life.

We recognise this non-existence in the *death of others*. The transformation of those who have just died, which announces that they have crossed the frontier of Hades, is the external counterpart of that transformation which we all gradually undergo and experience in the direction of death. Our internal experience finds an external support and justification. It announces itself in that 'echo' of which we have spoken. It is at the same time evoked and completed by the external experience, just as our idea of a fruit which we have known only in its unripe state is completed by the sight of the ripe fruit. Parmenides said that the dead body does not indeed perceive light or warmth or sounds because its fire has gone out but that it does perceive cold and silence and whatever else is opposed to them.[438] This cold and quiet, the state of being dead, is experienced by us only exceptionally. The dead experience it for ever. In them the world accomplishes and shows us the 'ripe fruit'.

Yet Epicurus too had right on his side when he said, 'When we are present, death is not present, and when death is present we are not.' The transformation is so thorough and complete that anyone who has undergone it is no longer the self that he was. Being dead means being quite other, the death direction is the direction towards the 'quite other'. This quite-other is contained in the world. It is a feature of the death-face of the world. It is what distinguishes it, together with all the gods which are its aspects and everyone of which represents a special face of the world, from mortal creatures. What makes the world 'quite other' is just this quality, that it supports non-existence lightly and eternally, while for living creatures it is the occasion of the most complete of all their transformations, so complete that it does not even exclude the notion of apotheosis, that the dead may become gods. Yet for living man the shock of the 'quite other' remains, for it includes also his own coming otherness. Here we encounter one of the fundamental elements of all religion, but only *one* among many.

The idea of non-existence as a world aspect is only *one* among many aspects of the universe to which it is related. First let us grasp the idea itself. It is evoked, or is echoed, in songs and stories, as ideas are evoked, not as a sum of internal and external experiences, but as a unity. It is the unity of our own death, cherished and ripening in us, and of the world's death towards which every living creature is moving and which in our own death concerns us too. Thus it is expressed in a song of the Dinka by the Upper Nile:[439]

> On the day when God created all things,
>> he created the sun
> and the sun rises and sets and returns again,
>> he created the moon
> and the moon rises and sets and returns again,
>> he created the stars
> and the stars rise and set and return again,
>> he created man
> and man comes forth, goes into the earth,
>> and does not return again.

That is the death-face of the world which it turns to men. This face intruded also into the maize festival of the Cora Indians. 'They appear only once, my younger brethren. Do they not die really for ever? But I never die, I shall appear continually.' Such an intrusion of the death-face of the world does not have the effect of something alien in the festive atmosphere. Where divinity is present to man, this difference too is present—mortality in its purest form, a form of non-existence contrasted with the existence of the gods. This characteristic of the festal phenomenon corresponds to the festal character of the phenomenon of death.

The inherent festiveness of Nature, its eternal and periodic character, which makes Nature itself the primal calendar, the true festival calendar, also causes the death-face of the world to appear. Evidence of this is to be found not only in primitive poetry but also in the classics. The joy of life in Catullus's *Vivamus mea Lesbia* acquires a special festivity from the reminder which it gives of the death-face of the world. It has playful licence, intensity, and seriousness all at the same time:

> *Soles occidere et redire possunt,*
> *Nobis cum semel occidit brevis lux*
> *Nox est perpetua una dormienda.*
> 'Suns may set and still return,
> When our brief light has set, for us
> There's one perpetual night of sleep.'

For the classical treatment of the same divine appearance we have the two spring poems of Horace, *Solvitur acris hiems* and *Diffugere nives*. The experience of the divine found by the poet in the seasons of the year is realised not so much through the images of particular gods, or at any rate not only by this means, but in his concluding argument. It is particularly sharp and clear in the second poem:

> *Damna tamen celeres reparant caelestia lunae;*
> *nos ubi decidimus,*
> *quo pius Aeneas, quo Tullus dives et Ancus,*
> *pulvis et umbra sumus.*
> Swift-following moons make good their heavenly losses.
> When we are dead and gone
> the way of pious Aeneas, rich Tullus, Ancus,
> we'll be but dust and shade.

The death-face of the world is clear for all to see.

5

On the other hand, it is never or almost never this face alone by which man is confronted. The rising up of the death idea does not mean the sinking of the opposite idea which is necessarily connected with it, the idea of life.

By this we must understand not an abstraction, not a mere concept. Just as in the idea of death the reality of non-existence appears in one aspect of the world, its death-face, so in the idea of life there appears the reality of existence as an aspect of the world. If non-existence shows itself in this world as pure negation and privation, yet in this same experience, the experience of death, there accumulates on the other side everything that is positive, and the life face of the world comes into view. If all these positive things, light, heat, gaiety, sound, did not evoke the idea of life, then there would be in the world no mode of appearance for death at all, there would be no 'idea' for non-existence. And not only that! If by an experiment of thought we were to think life out of the world, then there would no longer be any force or power left for non-existence. If we had not known life, we should never have experienced the power of death. It is only by life that non-existence has been raised to the rank of a reality which appears in the world and is powerful there.

The one idea leads inevitably to the other. Life makes the idea of death possible, even powerful, and the idea of death enables life in all its reality, its strength and power, to become actual. As the room for livable life steadily contracts about every mortal creature, our first thought might be that the grey and gloomy colours would increasingly dominate his landscape. But it is rather the other way round. The contraction causes all the colours of life, all that the world has to show, to glow more brightly.[440] The experience of this polarity may vary from one individual to another. The *fact* that it is experienced is just as much an ingredient of the structure of all living things, and consequently of the structure of the world, as the death direction. And it is not merely an external and literal manifestation, in which the idea of life and the idea of death appear together as the colourful splendour of the world. It is an aspect of the world in which we can fully participate without distinguishing between external vision and internal experience. To the slumbering and fitful consciousness of life the idea of death comes at times like water thrown on a dying fire, at times like oil to stir it into a blaze.

Yet this idea of life, the reality which so to speak blazes up in its fullest intensity under the pressure of death, is not to be confused with notions of another world. It is an essence, really existent and irreplaceable. We experience it simply as life, undiluted by its no less real opposite. Indeed we only experience what real existence is when we face that condition which is its total negation—the state of death. And this thing whose place can be taken only by something other, never by something like, is in truth irreplaceable.

6

The ideas of ancient religion, like the idea of death or the idea of life, are not only themselves aspects of the world, but also have various aspects of their own. We have only to consider in how many deities the life-aspect of the world appears. And the negation of existence in death, the pure privation of non-existence, may well be repugnant to us in comparison with all the positive gifts of life, its feelings and experience. Yet life too can be so painful and agonising that the purely negative aspect, the world of Hades, may appear mild and beneficent by contrast. There is a natural fear of death, and death is bitter for it. But there is also, just as natural, our urge towards death, which can build itself up into a longing for death. For this longing non-existence is sweet, and the mild and beneficent face of non-existence corresponds to it.

The bitterness and the sweetness of death are both realities. Poets give accounts of them as credible as those they give of love. Death was listed as one of the muses of great lyric poetry.[441] This was doubtless the case, too, in the period we are considering, though we have lost the choral songs which were sung in honour of Persephone, the goddess of death. But the *fact* that she is beautiful, though she may also be the sender of the dreaded Gorgon head,[442] should give students of religion food for thought. We should learn from the ancient artists and more recent poets that there is more in the case than a wish for some outward embellishment of death. True, students of religion are more inclined to follow natural science than poetry, but that would lead us here into a blind alley.

For natural science, natural death is really inconceivable. Anthropology has taught us that there are primitive peoples who are unwilling to consider death as a natural end.[443] Even in cases of natural death they look for an evil will which was the cause of death. This remarkable attitude can be explained psychologically. It is always tempting to explain away an unpleasant and well-known fact by a lie. One such fact is our inevitable natural death. Moreover, psychic research has drawn attention to the fact that even in cases of natural death the survivors have a feeling of guilt. The separation of a living creature from life appears always as an injustice of which we are helpless spectators. The propitiation of the dead is found among the mourning ceremonies of many societies. We can easily understand how the guilt may be pushed off on to some foreign magician.

On the other hand, there is nothing which could excuse the student of religion from concerning himself with that human behaviour in the face of death which is *really felt* as death. To do this, he is not absolutely obliged to make use of the experiences of poets. Psychology and biology have arrived at a common conclusion [444] that there is not only a life instinct—

and the fear of death bound up with it—but also a death instinct. The existence of this instinct follows from the structure of the living creature. 'Life instinct' and 'death instinct' are nothing but scientific terms for the fact that every living thing is continually in process of construction and destruction. These two, construction and destruction, can be thought of as two tracks, one directed upwards, the other downwards. But both together coincide with the direction of death. Construction proceeds just as much in the direction of death as destruction. It is really only *one* track, along which the living creature moves, and no one can tell at what point of life the movement begins to go downward. From the beginning the track is a track and not a stopping place. It is the track of life and therewith also the slope of death. 'Movement', 'track', 'slope', are obvious metaphors. Their real meanings are: 'movement'—'life'; 'life track'—'keeping oneself alive'; 'slope of death'—'giving oneself over to death'.[445]

Life and death instinct together, inseparably joined to one another, make up the nature of the living creature. They are two aspects of the living creature, which could just as well be called the 'dying creature'. In one and the same individual the 'dying creature' can even assume the predominance over the 'living creature'—in advanced years or in illness or, what is not the same, in tragic circumstances. Both creatures which make up the *one* living-dying creature, have their own fears and longings—fear of death and longing for life, fear of life and longing for death. The bitterness of death is connected with the first pair, the sweetness of death with the second.

Both are possible because man as a living and dying creature is in continual, structural contact with his own death, and yet has no direct experience of it as an actual state. Only the dead man experiences the state of death. However, we have the possibility of hurrying ahead along the track which is both the track of life and the slope of death and anticipating the end, not in reality but in dream and imagination. But there is a reason even for the anxious and wishful pictures of a dreaming or imagining mind. The reason is given by the track, which is at the same time a slope and has for its end an unwished-for, even terrifying, break, which can yet appear as a longed-for goal. But however this end may appear to the anticipating soul, whether dreadful or longed-for, the subject matter of the pictures in which it shows itself cannot be taken from death itself. Non-existence contains nothing.

That being-other is something different from any experience of life. Thus it is that even those fancies which make death seem pleasant come from life. The end is so imagined as if it were a continuation, wished for or not.

Such an 'as if', felt by everyone whether they admit it or no, sets a clear distinction between all notions of another world and the memories and experiences we have of the real world. Behind the experiences of life there stands the world as an uninterrupted, continuous background, here and now and always. Notions of another world are strictly no more than imaginative projections of the soul as, questioning and fearful, it anticipates the end. They take the soul into the 'other world', the world 'beyond' the end, which it has not yet reached. The background to such notions is neither this world nor that 'other world', for they do not refer to this world, which is here and now, and the other world to which they do refer is not here and now. That is why notions of the Beyond can never be confused with the knowledge that everyone has in himself about life—unless perhaps in exceptional states of ecstasy. But whence could such notions be generated if not from the storehouse of the soul and from possibilities of the mind, all of which form part of the content of this world?

In preference to the dreadful aspect of death we choose, quite naturally and unconsciously, its other, seductive aspect. The horrors of death are partly the fears of the soul as it anticipates the end. They are partly due, here and now, to the fact that the advance of privation and negation, that aspect of the world in which death shows itself, is in fact horrifying. To set against the fears of the soul we have its pleasant expectations and longings. These are as well founded as the fears and like them have a deep-lying cause and are supported by a real aspect of the world. For the natural inclination towards death of every living creature is balanced by the soul's capacity for self-deception, here stimulated by the fear of death itself. Thus hopes of another world arise, with sounds and colours more compelling than anything else the soul can dream of, even in its finest and deepest moments.

It is characteristic of other-world notions that even the most seductive among them are not powerful enough to prevent the dread aspect of death from presenting itself as a possibility which we ourselves shall perhaps escape, but to which *others* will all the more certainly fall victim. In this unequal distribution of the other world the demand for justice has played a varying part. It depends on the particular ethical mission of the religion to which

P

the promise of an after-life belongs. Alongside 'Paradiso' even in antiquity there stands 'Inferno', to satisfy the requirement of an unavoidable polarity. Not till the terrors of death had been philosophically 'overcome' were the soul's anxieties, at least in theory, removed. In this case, it is true, the loss of 'Inferno' has entailed that of 'Paradiso' too. Other-world notions of this crude kind, however, were in ancient religion secondary or peripheral phenomena. What is primary and central from the viewpoint of ancient religion is the comprehension of the reality of death, its complete acknowledgement, not its anticipatory veiling with pictures, dreadful or pleasant, of another world. It was this acknowledgement which figured in the cults of the ancient death deities.

7

Objective non-existence, realised in the death of living creatures, has appeared to us, as it necessarily did also to the ancients, in two aspects, as a dreaded end, and as a confining framework for all living creatures, on which they begin and on which, just as naturally, they cease to exist, as if arrived at a destination down a pleasant slope. On the other hand, for ancient man non-existence had another characteristic, different from those with which we are familiar. The modern idea of non-existence is completely empty. For ancient religious man non-existence, as the enclosing framework of organic life, was both full and empty at the same time.

It is not a logically bounded, exactly defined idea, like the non-existence of the philosophers, but a reality bordering on all living things. It is only in its border region that it can be comprehended at all, for its real core remains the inconceivable. In its border region, however, we do approach this inconceivable. We do it by intermediate stages, just as we approach non-existence. Between the light of day and the complete absence of light, for which the Greeks had the name Erebos, there is night. Before the fully formed state of an organism there is the germ. As ground of every living movement there is the resting earth. But where is the frontier between night, the germinal state, the earth in motherly repose, and a realm of non-existence conceived as lightless, germless, and *totally* dead?

We can indicate a domain of reality lying midway, so to speak, between the domain of wholly negative, pure non-existence and the domain of total existence, containing within itself every stage and every possibility. This intermediate realm of all the small life that swarms in darkness is the bottom-most layer in the great realm of life.[446] As the domain of incompleteness and motherly protection it is not closed to the realm of non-existence. For ancient man, indeed, it was so much a part of this realm that non-existence itself was joined to it. For non-existence could not be conceived as a sheer yawning void, but only as completely and inseparably bound up with the idea of mother earth and as one of her aspects. Thus it was that the fullness of germination itself became an aspect of non-existence.

We may speak here of a root aspect of existence.[447] 'The roots of the earth and of the sea', the two realms of swarming and germinating creatures, according to Hesiod[448] would be visible to the Titans in Tartaros if it were not for the total darkness called Erebos. It is a motherly domain which bore the world and now supports it and is always capable of bearing it anew. In terms of the labyrinth idea, the endless line of life, it is a stage before and after life. It was only for the philosopher among the Greeks, and not before him, that pure non-existence could be separated from existence, the *me on* from the *on*. Ancient religion worshipped the gods of heaven and of the underworld, the Olympic and the Chthonic deities. Their world was even more of a single whole than the world of later pantheistic philosophy. Non-existence had its place in it as a reality of the soul, a 'being-other' for man. In it both existence and non-existence were equally powerful, and capable of appearing in a rout of divine figures which surrounded and penetrated the universal whole with radiance and meaning.

NOTES

1 K. Reinhardt, *Platos Mythen* (Bonn, 1927).
2 Plato, *Republic*, 392b.
3 *ibid.*, 380c.
4 *ibid.*, 501; *Laws*, 752a.
5 Plato, *Republic*, 392a.
6 W. F. Otto, *Die Gestalt und das Sein* (Darmstadt, 1955), 68.
7 *Gottesfinsternis* (Zurich, 1953), 19.
8 *Myth in Primitive Psychology* (London, 1926).
9 Treated more fully in my *The Gods of the Greeks* (London and New York, 1957), 5.
10 *cf.* my 'Prometheus' in Rowohlt's *Deutsche Enzyklopädie* (Hamburg, 1959). Also Note 264, below.
11 *cf.* my *Apollon* (3rd ed., Düsseldorf, 1953), 271.
12 *cf.* my *Griechische Miniaturen* (Zurich, 1957), 77.
13 *cf.* my *Apollon, op. cit.*, 28.
14 A different 'state of the world' could equally be assumed and called 'Cosmos'; *cf.* K. Reinhardt, *Parmenides*, 174.
15 Due to Max Müller.
16 E. Cassirer, *The Philosophy of Symbolic Forms* (New Haven, 1953–57), II, 109.
17 G. van der Leeuw, *Religion in Essence and Manifestation. A Study in Phenomenology* (London, 1938. Sir Hedley Stewart Publ. no. 5).
18 *Epilegomena to the Study of Greek Religion* (Cambridge, 1921).
19 *Quaestiones Conviviales*, 6.8.
20 Phanodemos quoted by Athenaeus 456a.
21 *Faith, Hope and Charity in Primitive Religion* (Oxford, 1932).
22 *ibid.*, 39. The ceremony is exactly described by B. Spencer, *The Arunta* (1927), I, 194; *cf.* Notes 150 and 161.
23 For these corrections I am indebted to a great authority on the Arunta, Géza Róheim.
24 *cf.* Jung, Kerényi and Radin, *The Trickster* (London, 1956), 178.
25 G. Loeschke in *Ath. Mitt.* 19 (1894), 523; E. Buschor in *Ath. Mitt.* 53 (1928), 105; Kerényi in *Studi e Mat. di storia delle rel.* 9 (1933), 144.
26 *Das sterbende Afrika* (Frankfurt a.M., 1928), 259.

27 *Der religiöse Gehalt der Mythen* (Tübingen, 1933), 7.

28 *Die Nayarit-Expedition* I (Leipzig, 1912), 106.

29 *Homer und die klassische Philologie* (*Werke* III, 159; Munich, n.d.).

30 *cf.* J. Huizinga, *Homo Ludens*, of which the first Dutch edition appeared almost simultaneously with the first version of this chapter, the lecture 'Vom Wesen des Festes' in *Paideuma* I (1938), 59. In later editions Huizinga adopted my view of the nature of the festival.

31 *cf.* Father W. Schmidt, 'Spiele, Feste, Festspiele', in *Paideuma* 4 (1950), 11, who enlarges on the first version of this chapter. I attach no less importance to these distinctions than Father Schmidt, or than E. Jensen in his *Mythos und Kult bei Naturvölkern* (Wiesbaden, 1951), 61 *ff.*

32 The wording of this sentence is derived from a conversation with W. F. Otto.

33 *cf.* Robinson-Fluck, *A Study of the Greek Love-Names* (Baltimore, 1937), 6. As an addition to the deities and heroes there mentioned we have the Krater of Polygnotos from the Valle Trebba with its pair of gods, on which formerly ΕΚΛΟΕ was mistakenly read for ΚΑΛΕ and ΙΑΚΟΣ for ΚΑΛΟΣ. (See Pl. 58.)

34 *cf.* my article 'Zeus and Hera' in *Saeculum* I (1950), 253; and for the Jupiter Cycle of sixty years, *Klio* 29 (1936), 16.

35 Pausanias 1.28.10.

36 Porphyry *De Abst.* 2.30; the two most thorough analyses of this rite, L. Deubner, *Attische Feste*, 158, and W. F. Otto in *Paideuma* 4 (1950), 111, pay no special attention to this important detail.

37 *cf.* my article 'Dramatische Gottesgegenwart in der griechischen Religion' in *Eranos Jahrbuch* 29 (1950), 25; *Dioniso* 1950, Nos. 3–4.

38 Plutarch *De Is. et Os.* 35; *Quaest Gr.* 36.

39 Dionysos in my *The Gods of the Greeks*, 254; Pelops in my *The Heroes of the Greeks*, 59; Aison, Jason, Pelias, *ibid.*, 273 *ff.*; Orpheus, *ibid.*, Pl. 65; Itys, *ibid.*, 289; children of Thyestes, *ibid.*, 305.

40 *cf.* my study 'Die Herkunft der Dionysosreligion' in *Arbeitsgemeinschaft für Forschung des Landes Nordrhein-Westfalen* 58 (1956), and my book *Der frühe Dionysos* (Oslo, 1961).

41 This is an unscientific generalization of the ideas of two original theologians, Rudolf Otto in his *The Idea of the Holy* (London, 1950), and Gerardus van der Leeuw in his *Phänomenologie der Religion*.

42 6.56.6. Polybius calls the *religio* of the Romans *deisidaimonía* and in speaking of it uses the verb *ektragodeín*, which with him is derogatory.

43 *Athen.* 274a.

44 *De har. resp.* 19.

45 Is. xi, 2; *cf.* Robertson-Smith, *Lectures on the Religion of the Semites* (3rd ed., London, 1927), 23.

46 W. F. Otto, *Arch. Rel. Wiss.* 14 (1911), 104; *cf.* his first essay on the subject (*ibid.*, 12, 532), and the following chapters IV and VI.

47 *cf.* my article in *Byzant.-Neugriech. Jahrb.* 1931, 306 *ff.*, and J. C. A. van Herten, *Threskeia, Eulabeia, Hiketes* (Diss. Amsterdam, 1934), 28 *ff.*

48 Plato, *Laws* 879e; Demosth. 21.61; 59.74.

49 τὸ πιστεύειν σφόδρα and τῦφος.

50 Camillus 6.

51 Seeger in *Die Religion in Geschichte und Gegenwart* II, 1200.

52 According to *Theolegumena arithmeticae* ed. Ast, p. 60.25; Diels 32A13.

53 τὸ λίαν ἀπιστεῖν.

54 Herodotus 2.18; 37; 64; van Herten 2.

55 *cf.* W. F. Otto's essay, already quoted, on *religio* and *superstitio* in *Arch. f. Rel. Wiss.* 12, 532.

56 Charakt. 16; *cf.* H. Bolkestein, *Theophrastos' Charakter der Deisidaimonia als religionsgesch. Urkunde* (Giessen, 1929).

57 Polit. 1315a; for the history of the word, P. J. Koets, *Deisidaimonia* (Purmerend, 1929).

58 *cf.* Wilamowitz, *Glaube der Hellenen* I (Berlin, 1931), 362.

59 'That which is in habitual practice, use or possession' according to Liddell and Scott.

60 *cf.* H. E. Stier, *Nomos Basileus* (Diss. Rostock, 1927).

61 *Griechische Kulturgeschichte* I, 86. He quotes also the words of Demaratus to Xerxes (Herodot. I, 104) about the *despotes nomos*, the 'monarch Law', and recalls the worship of the law-givers of the Greek cities: a cult equivalent of the myth of the divine origin of Law, even when it comes from man.

62 Fr. 114 Diels.

63 Fr. 152 Bowra; *cf.* Stier, p. 5.

64 Fr. 24.15; *cf.* Stier, p. 8.

65 *Erga* 276; *cf.* Stier, p. 10.

66 Fr. 70 Bowra; Stier, p. 6.

67 Homer never speaks of *nómos* and *nomízein*.

68 *cf.* E. Willinger, *Hagios* (Giessen, 1922).

69 *Od.* 17.402.

70 *Il.* 14.261.

71 *Il.* 1.21; 5.434.

72 *Od.* 9.200.

73 *Il.* 1.23.

74 Pind. *Pyth.* 9.64.

75 *Od.* 5.123; 18.202; 20.71.

76 *Od.* 11.386.

77 *Od.* 21.259.

78 *Erga* 465.

79 W. F. Otto, *The Homeric Gods* (London, 1955), 83.

80 *cf.* Greek mythology's view of life as described in my *Prometheus*.

81 Weniger, p. 18.

82 U. v. Wilamowitz, *Der Glaube der Hellenen* (Berlin, 1931, 1932), I, 22; not to be regarded as certain, Wilamowitz being much given to premature categorical assertions.

83 See Note 81.

84 Rudolf Otto, *The Idea of the Holy* (London, 1950), 43; Van der Leeuw, *Phänomenologie der Religion*, 29.

85 W. F. Otto, *op. cit.*, 86 *ff.*; and especially in my *Apollon*, 3rd ed., 41, 61, concerning Apollo; also W. F. Otto in a posthumous article in *Paideuma* 7 (1959), 19.

86 *cf.* W. W. Fowler, *Roman Essays and Interpretations* (Oxford, 1920), 15 *ff.*

87 Festus, s.v. *homo sacer*; Fowler, p. 19.

88 *Topica* 90; *cf.* Fowler, *The Religious Experience of the Roman People* (London, 1922), 470, according to Nettleship, *Contributions to Latin Lexicography*, s.v. *sanctus*.

89 For the history of the word up to Theophrastus, *cf.* J. Ch. Bolkestein, *Hosios en Eusebes* (Amsterdam, 1936); an interpretation without drawing the necessary distinctions was given by H. Jeanmaire, in *Rev. des et. gr.* 58 (1945), 66 *ff.*

90 *Od.* 16.423; 22.412.

91 229–38; *cf.* my article in the periodical *Maia* (Rome) 4 (1950), 10 *ff.*

92 Hom. *Hymn. Cer.* 211.

93 Hom. *Hymn. Merc.* 130, 172–3, 469–70.

94 Soph. *Ant.* 1071, *cf.* 74.

95 Suidas s.v. ὁσία.

96 Theophr. in Porph. *de abst.* 27.403.

97 *Od.* 16.423.

98 Thus U. v. Wilamowitz, *Platon* I (Berlin, 1920), 61.

99 Eur. *Bacch.* 370 *ff.*

100 Eur. *Alc.* 10.

101 Plut. *Quaest. Gr.* 292d; *Def. or.* 437a; *Is. et Os.* 365a.

102 *cf.* Roscher, *Lex.*, s.v. Delphos; W. R. Halliday, *The Greek Questions of Plutarch* (Oxford, 1928), 57.

103 Verg. *Aen.* 5.80.

104 *Topica* 90.

105 Wilamowitz, *Glaube der Hellenen* I, 15 *f.*

106 Thus of childbirth, Aristoph. Lys. 743.

107 *cf.* Thuc. 2.52.4; J. Ch. Bolkestein, 168 *ff.*

108 Dig. 1.8.9.3.

109 *cf.* Plut. *Alex.* 31—the use of the intensive form ἱερουργίας ἱερουργούμενος.

110 U. v. Wilamowitz, *Glaube der Hellenen* I, 21 *f.*

111 *cf.* G. Link, *De vocis 'sanctus' usu pagano* (Diss. Königsberg, 1910), 17.

112 For the history of the concept: Wilamowitz, *op. cit.*; J. Ch. Bolkestein, *op. cit.*; O. Kern, *Die Religion der Griechen* I (Berlin, 1926). Not one of these three treatments is exhaustive.

113 *cf.* W. F. Otto in *Arch. Bel.-Wiss.* 12 (1909), 537; C. E. v. Erffa, 'Aidós', *Philologus* Suppl. 30, 2, 1937, 27.

114 *cf.* J. Rohr's 'Der okkulte Kraftbegriff im Altertum', *Philologus* Suppl. 17, 1, 1923.

115 σέβας μ' ἔχει εἰσορόωντα. *Od.* 3.123; 4.75; 142; 6.161.

116 Verse 10: σέβας τότε πᾶσι ἰδέσθαι/ἀθανάτοις τε θεοῖς κ.τ.λ.

117 σέβας δέ σε θυμὸν ἱκέσθω. *Il.* 18.178 *ff.*

118 σεβάσσατο γὰρ τό γε θυμῶι. *Il.* 6.167; 417.

119 οὔ νυ σέβασθε; *Il.* 4.242 *f.*

120 Verse 10: θαυμαστὸν γανόωντα.

121 Aesch. *Suppl.* 755; *Cho.* 644.

122 θαῦμα ἰδέσθαι *Il.* 5.725 and elsewhere; θάμβος δ' ἔχειν εἰσορόωντας *Il.* 4.79 at the sight of a sign in which Pallas Athene conceals herself but which remains opaque and without symbolic meaning.

123 This is directed at A.-J. Festugière.

124 Hes. *Theog.* 44.

125 R. Schulz, 'Aidós' (Diss. Rostock, 1910); W. Jäger in *Paideia* I (Berlin, 1934), 28 *f.*; Erffa, *op. cit.*; W. J. Verdenius in *Mnemosyne* 3, 12 (1945), 47 *ff.*

126 Ἕκτορ, τέκνον ἐμόν, τάδε τ' αἴδεο καὶ ἐλέησον
αὐτήν, εἴ ποτέ τοι λαθικηδέα μαζὸν ἐπέσχον·
τῶν μνῆσαι, φίλε τέκνον, ἄμυνε δὲ δήϊον ἄνδρα
τείχεος ἐντὸς ἐών . . . *Il.* 22.82 *ff.*

127 *Il.* 22.66 *ff.*

128 Farbenlehre § 916–17.

129 *cf.* my *Griechische Miniaturen* (Zurich, 1957), 27.

130 *Od.* 16.75; 19.527.

131 This, with the other Themis relationships, has escaped attention: *cf.* J. E.

Harrison, *Themis* (2nd ed., Cambridge, 1927) and further literature quoted by K. Latte, 'Themis', in *Paulys R.E.* 1934.

132 εἶδε τὰ μὴ θεμιτά. Call. *Hymn.* 5.78.

133 Theocr. 1.106/7 with the explanation given by U. v. Wilamowitz, *Textgeschichte der griechischen Bukoliker* (Berlin, 1906), 233 *f.*

134 Plin. *Nat. hist.* 36.20.

135 Chr. Blinkenberg, *Knidia* (Copenhagen, 1933), 36.

136 οὐκ εἶδεν ἃ μὴ θέμις. *Anth. Gr.* 16.160.5.

137 τὰ καὶ θέμις. *Anth. Gr.* 16.180.5.

138 ὅσα μὴ θέμις ὁρᾶσθαι. Anacreontica 55.10 Hiller.

139 *Il.* 11.134.

140 *Il.* 20.4; *Od.* 2.64.

141 Hom. *Hymn. Ap.* 541.

142 Erffa, *op. cit.*, 19, 49, etc.

143 'Union without Themis.' Scholion in Lycophr. 1141 concerning Ajax and Cassandra.

144 W. F. Otto in *Arch. Rel.-Wiss.* 14 (1911), 413, 1.

145 For the later history of the term *cf.* Th. Ulrich, *Pietas (pius) als politischer Begriff im römischen Staate bis zum Tode des Kaisers Commodus* (Diss. Breslau, 1930).

146 Dio Cassius fr. 95, 1 (Ulrich, pp. 2, 3); Plut. *Cam.* 24; Agis 20 (van Herten, 41).

147 Cic. *Har. resp.* 19; Lact. 4.3; Fowler rel. Exp. 462.

148 G. Wissowa, *Religion und Kultus der Römer* (2nd ed. Munich, 1912), 331.

149 For reasons of a stricter prosody; Fowler, *op. cit.*, 412.

150 Plin. *Nat. hist.* 7.121; Val. Max. 5.4.7.

151 Val. Max. 5.4 ext. 1; Hygin *fab.* 242, the history of Mykon and Pero, a story which could also have originated in the Roman legend. Either direction of migration is quite possible.

152 Festus, p. 209.

153 αἰδέομαι Τρῶας καὶ Τρωάδας ἑλκεσιπέπλους. *Il.* 22.106; 6.442.

154 νέμεσις δέ μοι ἐξ ἀνθρώπων ἔσσεται. *Od.* 2.136/7.

155 Erffa, *op. cit.*, 30 *ff.*, 50 *f.* and 54.

156 *cf.* P. Kretschmer in *Glotta* 13, 106.

157 *Theog.* 223–4; *Erga* 197 *ff.*

158 *cf.* my essay 'Die Geburt der Helena' in *Albae Vigiliae N.F.* III (Zurich, 1945), 9.

159 Kypria fr. XXIII Allen.

160 Erffa, 29 *f.*

161 *Il.* 3.227; *Od.* 9.109.

162 This is a consequence of the facts given by W. F. Otto in *Paideuma* 7 (1959), 20 *ff*.

163 *Il.* 16.388.

164 οὐδὲ θεῶν ὄπιν αἰδέσατ' οὐδὲ τράπεζαν. *Od.* 21.28.

165 W. F. Otto in *Arch. Rel.-Wiss.* 14, 421.

166 190.

167 479.

168 480; Pind. fr. 121 Bowra; Soph. fr. 837 Pearson.

169 *cf.* my article 'Über das Geheimnis der eleusinischen Mysterien', in *Paideuma* 7 (1959), 69, and my book, published in Dutch, *Eleusis* (The Hague, 1960).

170 *Il.* 9.186–89.

171 20.131 χαλεποὶ δὲ θεοὶ φαίνεσθαι ἐναργεῖς.

172 16.161 οὐ γάρ πω πάντεσσι θεοὶ φαίνονται ἐναργεῖς.

173 *Il.* 5.127.

174 O. Jörgensen in *Hermes* 39 (1904), 357 *ff.*; E. Hedén, *Homerische Götterstudien* (Diss. Uppsala, 1912).

175 W. F. Otto, *The Homeric Gods*, 169–228.

176 The history of the word before Plato in A. E. Taylor, *Varia Socratica*, I. ser. (Oxford, 1911), 178 *ff.*

177 *cf.* my article 'MYΘOE in verbaler Form', *Festschrift W. Szilasi* (Berne, 1960), 121.

178 *cf.* B. Snell, 'Die Ausdrücke für den Begriff des Wissens in der vorplatonischen Philosophie', in *Phil. Unters.* 29 (1924), 20 *ff.*; J. Böhme, *Die Seele und das Ich im homerischen Epos* (Leipzig, 1929), 24.

179 W. Jaeger, *Aristoteles* (Berlin, 1923), 83.

180 980a.

181 Snell, 26 *f.*

182 *cf.* Plat. *Tim.*, 47a.

183 The following examples: *Il.* 24.41; *Od.* 9.189; 3.277.

184 *Topika* 8.1246b; W. F. Otto, *The Gods of the Greeks*, 179.

185 Sext. Emp. *c. phys.* 1.23, p. 242 Mutschmann; *cf.* Plut. *Aem. Paul.* 3 and Cic. *De Nat. Deor.* 1.116.

186 *cf.* W. Jaeger, *The Theology of the Early Greek Philosophers* (Oxford, 1947).

187 983a.

188 *cf.* my article 'Das Theta von Samothrake', in *Geist und Werk*, Festschrift D. Brody (Zurich, 1958), 129.

189 *Il.* 15.422; 24.294; *cf.* A. Fulda, *Inters. üb. d. Sprache der hom. Gedichte* I (Duisburg, 1865); Böhme, *op. cit.*, 24.

190 *Erga* 257.

191 *cf.* K. Riezler, *Parmenides* (Frankfurt a.M., 1934), 64.
192 Böhme, 24 *ff.*
193 *Il.* 15.80; *Od.* 7.36.
194 *Od.* 2.382, etc.
195 686; *cf.* Böhme, 54.
196 *Il.* 19.9.
197 *Il.* 5.874; 15.41.
198 *Od.* 1.349; 6.189; *cf. Od.* 1.32.
199 *Il.* 1.5; *cf.* Böhme 58.
200 *Il.* 15.461 with the explanation of P. Philippson, *op. cit.*, 27, 7.
201 *Od.* 5.104.
202 14.294; *cf.* Böhme 54.
203 *Il.* 19.91–113.
204 Parm. fr. 6 Diels with the explanation of Riezler, *op. cit.*
205 *cf.* Boll, *Vita contemplativa* 32 (*Kleine Schr. z. Sternkunde des Altertums*, Leipzig, 1950, 303 *ff.*); Jaeger, *Aristoteles*, 99 *f.*
206 *cf.* my article 'Das Theta von Samothrake', 131.
207 *cf.* P. Boesch, 'ΘΕΩΡΟΣ' (Berlin, 1908).
208 *cf.* Ziehen in Pauly-Wissowa's *Realenc.*
209 327b.
210 Prom. 118; 302.
211 Hdt. 1.29; 3.32; Democr. fr. 191; 194.
212 Fr. 11 Diels.
213 Ast: *Index Plat.*
214 *Eth. Nic.* 10.7; *cf. Metaph.* 1072b 14–40.
215 *cf.* Boll, *op. cit.*, 22 *f.*; Aristot. fr. 58 Rose.
216 Fr. 481 according to Boll 23.
217 *cf.* my *Apollon* (3rd ed.), 241 *ff.*
218 *cf.* my *Griechische Miniaturen* (Zurich, 1957), 27 *ff.*
219 Schol. Pind. *Pyth.* 4.151b.
220 *Orator* 9.27.
221 Fr. 12 Diels.
222 2.2; so far as concerns the *mens deorum* confirmed by E. Norden, *Aus altrömischen Priesterbüchern* (Lund, 1939), 282.
223 *cf.* the edition of J. B. Mayor, III, p. xxiv.
224 According to *Erga* 42 in Eus. *Praep. evang.* 14.5.15.
225 *cf.* Snell, *op. cit.*, 2.
226 *Metaph.* 8.10.
227 Diog. *Laert.* 4.62.

228 Thomas Mann in respect of Pope Pius XII.

229 *cf.* R. Reitzenstein, *Hellenistische Mysterienreligionen* (3rd ed., Leipzig and Berlin, 1927), 252, and my remark in *Arch. Rel.-Wiss.* 12, 552 *ff.*

230 *De divinatione* 1.2.

231 Gellius 4.9.5.

232 In Gellius, *op. cit.*

233 W. F. Otto in *Arch. Rel.-Wiss.* 12, 552.

234 *cf.* F. Altheim, *A History of Roman Religion* (London, 1938), 411.

235 E. R. Dodds, *The Greeks and the Irrational* (Univ. of California Press, 1951), index; *cf.* Rostowtzew in *Clio* 16, 203, and my book *Die griechische-orientalische Romanliteratur* (Tübingen, 1927), 97.

236 Van der Leeuw, *Phänomenologie der Religion*, 366.

237 Thus van der Leeuw, who quotes the verse from Dante, *Par.*, 29.12.

238 *Erga* 802.

239 2.53.

240 *cf.* T. B. L. Webster, *From Mycenae to Homer* (London, 1958).

241 The study of Ventris and Chadwick, 'Evidence for Greek dialect in the Mycenaean archives', in *J. Hell. Stud.* 73 (1953), 84, is now out of date.

242 *cf.* my study 'Die Herkunft der Dionysos-Religion', in *Arbeitsgemeinschaft für Forschung Nordrhein-Westfalen* 58 (1956), and my book *Der frühe Dionysos* (Oslo, 1961).

243 *cf.* my *Streifzüge eines Hellenisten* (Zurich, 1960), p. 45.

244 Van der Leeuw, *op. cit.*, 327.

245 In his *Dionysos*, 41.

246 Otto, *Dionysos*, 40, and my remarks on the leap from the Leukas cliffs in *Arch. Rel.-Wiss.* 24, 61; also Kinross, Kerényi and Hoegler, *Greece in Colour*, for the plate, 'The cliffs of Leukas'.

247 *cf.* my *Umgang mit Göttlichem* (Göttingen, 1955), 34.

248 *cf.* above, pp. 69 *f.*

249 *cf.* S. Eitrem, *Beiträge zur griech. Religionsgesch.* III (Kristiania, 1920), 44 *ff.*; L. Deubner, 'Ololyge und Verwandtes', in *Abh. Akad. Berlin* 1941.

250 P. Stengel, *Griech. Kultusaltertümer* (Munich, 1890), 112.

251 Schwenn, *op. cit.*, 100.

252 W. F. Otto in *Paideuma* 4 (1950), 111.

253 K. Th. Preuss, *Die geistige Kultur der Naturvölker*, 38.

254 Fr. Cumont, *Die Mysterien des Mithra* (2nd ed.), 122.

255 Stengel in *Hermes* 29, 391; H. v. Fritze, *ibid.* 32, 235; Ziehen, *ibid.* 37, 391; Stengel, *ibid.* 38, 41, 230; *Kultusalt.* 110; Eitrem, *Opferreitung und Voropfer* (Kristiania, 1915), 261.

256 Above, pp. 57 *f.*

257 Athen. 192b.

258 Stengel, *Kultusalt.* 105.

259 L. Weniger in *Arch. Rel.-Wiss.* 22, 16 *ff.*

260. *Jer.* xxiii, 23–24.

261 H. v. Fritze in *Arch. Jahrb.* 18 (1903), 58.

262 Apollo, 'the far god': W. F. Otto, *The Homeric Gods*, 63 *f.*; Dionysos 'the arriving god': Otto, *Dionysos*, 75 *ff.*; my *Griechische Miniaturen*, 119 *ff.*

263 *Dionysos*, 23.

264 *cf.* my *Prometheus*, in Rowohlt's *Deutsche Enzyklopädie* (Hamburg, 1959), 95; this appeared in English as Vol. 1 of my *Archetypal Images of Greek Religion* (London and New York, 1962).

265 Hom *Il.* 1.424–5; *Od.* 1.22 *ff.*; 7.201 *ff.*

266 *Ol.* 11.13; *Pyth.* 10.40; *Nem.* 1.17, together with my remarks in *Hermes* 66, 424.

267 P. Philippson, *Untersuchungen über den griech. Mythos* (Zurich, 1944), 37. The following quotation: fr. 82 Rz. *cf.* Paus. 8.2.4; Cat. 64, 384–6.

268 *Gen.* xviii.

269 *cf.* Reitzenstein-Schäder, *Studien zum antiken Synkretismus* (Leipzig, 1926), 58.

270 *Erga* 108.

271 Eduard Meyer, *Kleine Schriften* II, 35.

272 *Nem.* 6.1.

273 *cf.* my *The Gods of the Greeks*, 209 (p. 184 in the Pelican edition).

274 *Erga* 144–5.

275 *Theog.* 563; the original reading was probably μελίοισι.

276 *Theog.* 183–7.

277 *Od.* 7.60; *The Gods of the Greeks*, 28 (Pelican ed., 24).

278 *Erga* 175; Reitzenstein, *op. cit.*, 62.

279 Riezler, *Parmenides*, 47; W. Luther, '*Wahrheit*' und '*Lüge*' im ältesten Griechentum (Borna-Leipzig, 1935), 12; *Philol. Wochenschr.* 1937, 973.

280 *Theog.* 17; 137 etc.: ἀγκυλομήτης.

281 ἀγκύλη.

282 *cf.* Jung, Kerényi and Radin, *The Trickster* (London, 1956), 181.

283 *Erga* 59.

284 *cf.* E. Drerup, *Homerische Poetik* (Würzburg, 1921), 414 *ff.*

285 *Gen.* xviii, 27.

286 R. Otto, *The Idea of the Holy*, p. 9.

287 Insofar as the 'sardonic laughter' was the laughter of the Asia Minor god Sanda: Höfer in *Roschers Lex.* IV, 327.

288 *cf.* H. Zimmer, *Maya* (Stuttgart, 1936), 468; in contrast to the Homeric laughter of the gods, P. Friedländer, *Die Antike* 10, 209.

289 A. Dieterich, *Abraxas* (Leipzig, 1891), 17 *f.*, and E. Norden, *Die Geburt des Kindes*, 66 *f.*

290 *Erga* 159 *ff.*

291 *cf.* my *Apollon* (3rd ed., Düsseldorf, 1953), 123.

292 *Il.* 22.168 *ff.*

293 Jean Paul, *Vorschule der Aesthetik* § 30, cited by Friedländer.

294 Friedländer, *Die Antike* 10, 226.

295 584 *ff.*

296 Aesch. *Prom.* 14; 39; L. R. Farnell, *The Cults of the Greek States* V, 381.

297 *cf.* my *Prometheus*, p. 34, and *Geistiger Weg Europas* (Zurich, 1955), pp. 38 *ff.*

298 *Od.* 8.267 *ff.*

299 347.

300 W. F. Otto, *The Homeric Gods*, 244.

301 Otto, *op. cit.*, 244.

302 307.

303 Diogenian 8.47

304 *cf.* my *Prometheus, op. cit.*

305 Fr. V. Allen.

306 389–90.

307 According to Schelling; *cf.* Friedländer, *op. cit.*, 210.

308 *Il.* 491; 508.

309 426.

310 *Il.* 20.21.

311 *Il.* 19.404 *ff.*

312 Hesych. s.v. τίταξ and τιτῆναι; or 'fathers'—J. Sundwall in my *Prometheus*, 34, 3.

313 *Theog.* 124 *f.*

314 Stengel, *Kultusaltertümer*, 151.

315 G. Wissowa, *Religion und Kultus der Römer* (2nd ed., Munich, 1912), 380.

316 *De nat. deor.* 1.116; *Part. orat.* 78.

317 *cf.* W. Warde Fowler, *The Religious Experience of the Roman People*, 24 *ff.*

318 Wissowa, *op. cit.*; Fowler, *op. cit.*

319 *cf.* K. Vahlert, *Praedeismus und römische Religion* (Frankfurter Diss., Limburg a. d. Lahn, 1935).

320 *cf.* L. R. Taylor in *Classical Studies in Honour of J. C. Rolfe* (Philadelphia, 1931), 305 *ff.*; Vahlert, *op. cit.*, 26.

321 Wissowa, *op. cit.*, 26.

322 C. Koch, *Der römische Juppiter* (Frankfurt a. M., 1937), 30.

323 *Ant. Rom.* 2.19.
324 Sir J. G. Frazer, *The Golden Bough* (3rd ed.), VI, 227 *ff*.
325 H. J. Rose, *The Roman Questions of Plutarch* (Oxford, 1924), 111.
326 H. J. Rose, *op. cit.*, 112.
327 'Having nothing else to do'; Rose, *op. cit.*
328 Gell. *Noct. Att.* 10.15.16: *Dialis quotidie feriatus est.*
329 On the term, G. Rohde, *Die Kultsatzungen der röm. Pontifices* (Berlin, 1936), 27, and Wagenvoort in *Glotta* 26, 115.
330 Fest. Paul. p. 224.
331 Serv. in Verg. *Georg.* 1.31.
332 Wissowa, *op. cit.*, 506, 5.
333 Macr. *Sat.* 2.2; 7.3; *cf. meridialis* from *meridies* Gell. 2.22.14.
334 *De Ling. Lat.* 5.66.
335 Liv. 36.53.7; Koch, *op. cit.*, 88 *f.*
336 Dion. Hal. *Ant. Rom.* 2.10.3; Wissowa, *op. cit.*, 237.
337 Gell. 5.12.12; Altheim, *A History of Roman Religion*, 262.
338 *cf.* Koch, *op. cit.*, 67 *ff.*
339 Gell. 10.15.24 *f.*
340 Gell. 10.15.3.
341 Cass. Dio 43.24.4; Wissowa, *op. cit.*, 145.
342 Serv. in Verg. *Aen.* 8.552; Tac. *Ann.* 3.58; Wissowa, *op. cit.*, 505.
343 Gell. 10.15.25.
344 Gell. 10.15.12; Plut. *Quaest. Rom.* 111.
345 *cf.* my article 'Herr der wilden Tiere?' in *Symb. Osl.* 33 (1957), 127.
346 Gell., *op. cit.*; Plut., *op. cit.*, 110; Koch 36.2.
347 Gell. 10.15.19; Plut., *op. cit.*, 109.
348 Gell., *op. cit.*; Plut., *op. cit.*, 11 *f.*; Koch, *op. cit.*
349 *cf.* my 'Gedanken über Dionysos', in *Studie e mat. di stor. delle rel.* 11 (1935), 34.
350 Gell. 10.15.13; Plut. *Quaest. Rom.* 112.
351 *Ov. Fasti* 2.282.
352 Varro *De Ling. Lat.* 6.16; Wissowa, *op. cit.*, 118.
353 *cf.* Rohde, *op. cit.*, 112.
354 Plin. *Nat. Hist.* 18.10; Wissowa, *op. cit.*, 118.
355 Gell. 10.15.5.
356 Gell. 10.19.9.
357 Gell. 10.15.6.
358 Gell. 10.15.8.
359 Gell. 10.15.8.

360 For the kinds of trees *cf.* Macr. Sat. 3.20; C. O. Thulin, *Die etruskische Disziplin* II (Gothenburg, 1909), 94 *ff.*; Rohde, *op. cit.*, 168.

361 Ov. *Fasti* 3.429 *ff.* The mere sight of him released the condemned from punishment. He so to speak carried the right of asylum around with him: Gell. 10.15.10.

362 Dion. Hal. *Ant. Rom.* 2.10.3; Wissowa 237; Koch 78.

363 *cf.* E. Samter, *Familienfeste der Griech. u. Röm.* (Berlin, 1901), 33.

364 As an ancient Italian form of Jupiter, Veiovis belongs to the same type as the Jupiter of Praeneste and Jupiter Anxurus, perhaps the type of the 'divine child'; *cf.* my discussion in Jung and Kerényi, *Introduction to a Science of Mythology* (London, 1951), 87.

365 *Iovis fiducia dicitur*, Macr. Sat. 1.15.

366 Gaius 1.112; Wissowa 119.

367 Wissowa, *op. cit.*, 118.

368 Fest. Paul. p. 115; transmitted as *Dispiter*.

369 Wissowa, *op. cit.*, 119.

370 *Coniunx sancta Dialis.*

371 Ov. *Fasti* VI, 226; Festus p. 92; Rose, *op. cit.*, 110.

372 Festus p. 92; Rose, *op. cit.*, 110.

373 Plut. *Quaest. Rom.* 86.

374 H. Diels, *Sibyllinische Blätter* (Berlin, 1890), 43, 2.

375 Macr. Sat. 1.15.18–20.

376 Prop. 4.8.3.

377 Koch, *op. cit.*, 103 *ff.*

378 The temple of 'Veiovis *in insula*' was dedicated on the Kalends of January, that of 'Veiovis *inter duos lucos*' on the Nones after the Kalends of March (which were particularly sacred to Juno Lucina).

379 F. Altheim in *Klio* 30 (1937), 51.

380 Tib. 4.6.1.

381 Varro *De Ling. Lat.* 5.6; Festus p. 369 Lindsay.

382 H. J. Rose in *Folk-Lore* 47 (1936), 397 *f.*

383 Serv. in Verg. *Aen.* 3.607.

384 CIL IX 3513 from a temple of Juppiter Liber; *cf.* Altheim, *Griech. Götter im alten Rom* (Giessen, 1939), 47; *Terra Mater* 24 *f.*

385 Gell. 10.15.22 *f.*

386 Frazer, *op. cit.*

387 Serv. in Verg. *Aen.* 4.29.

388 Tac. *Ann.* 3.58.71.

389 Gell. 10.15.16 *f.*

390 Appian 1.74; *cf.* K. Sauer, *Untersuchungen zur Darstellung des Todes* (Diss. Frankfurt, 1930), 42.

391 Gell. 10.15.7.

392 Gell. 10.15.7.

393 Gell. 10.15.14.

394 Juvenal 6.22.

395 Gell. 10.15.14.

396 *Apud eius lecti fulcrum capsulam esse cum strue atque ferto oportet* (the preceding *neque* must have been interpolated, contrary to the sense).

397 Liv. 5.52.13.

398 *de eo lecto trinoctium continuum non decubat*, Gell., *op. cit.*

399 C. Koch, *Gestirnverehrung im alten Italien* (Frankfurt a. M.), 98 *ff.*

400 W. Staudacher, *Die Trennung von Himmel und Erde. Ein vorgriechischer Schöpfungsmythus* (Tübingen, 1942).

401 Quaest. Rom. III; ὥσπερ ἔμψυχον καὶ ἱερὸν καὶ ἄγαλμα.

402 *cf.* Tac. *Ann.* 3.71.

403 F. Altheim, *A History of Roman Religion* (London, 1938), 424.

404 W. F. Otto, *Die Gestalt und das Sein* (Darmstadt, 1955), 356.

405 Altheim, *op. cit.*

406 V. Niebergall, *Griechische Religion und Mythologie in der älteste Literatur der Römer* (Diss. Giessen, 1937), 16.

407 *cf.* Th. Mommsen, *Röm. Gesch.* I, 26 *f.*

408 C. Schmidt, 'Gespräche Jesu mit seinen Jüngern nach der Auferstehung', in *Text u. Unters.* 43, 455.

409 Erwin Rhode's once-famous work, *Psyche*, is now partly obsolete. It was made so by W. F. Otto, *Die Manen* (2nd ed., Darmstadt, 1958).

410 Plat. *Teaet.* 155d; Arist. *Met.* 982b.11.

411 *cf.* above, p. 113.

412 θαῦμα ἰδέσθαι.

413 'That deep shudder which we are too ready to call fear, whereas it may also be the expression of a most solemn and sublime mood.' W. F. Otto, *The Homeric Gods*, p. 143.

414 *Schriften aus dem Nachlass* I (Berlin, 1933), 8.

415 *cf.* G. Perthes, *Über den Tod* (2nd ed., Stuttgart, 1927).

416 *Sein und Zeit* I, 238.

417 *op. cit.*, 247.

418 *cf.* my *Labyrinth-Studien* (2nd ed., Zurich, 1950).

419 Fr. 48 and 15 Diels.

420 105c–e.

Q

421 *Ad Menec.* 125.

422 African examples in H. Baumann, *Schöpfung und Urzeit des Menschen im Mythos der afrikanischen Völker* (Berlin, 1936), 268 *ff.*; H. Abrahamsson, *The Origin of Death. Studies in African Mythology* (Uppsala, 1951).

423 *cf.* my article in *Hermes* 66 (1931), 418.

424 *cf.* E. Buschor in *Münchener Jahrb. bild. Künste* 2 (1925), 167 *ff.*

425 *Sein und Zeit* 239.

426 *op. cit.*, 240.

427 According to W. F. Otto, *The Homeric Gods*, 142 *ff.*, this 'having-been' *is* the Homeric Hades.

428 Cic. *De Nat. Deor.* 240.

429 The quotations are from the *Stundenbuch*.

430 *op. cit.*, 9 *ff.*

431 W. F. Otto's criticism of Scheler.

432 N. Berdyaev, *Freedom and the Spirit* (London, 1935), vii.

433 *cf.* my *Griechische Miniaturen*, 148 *ff.*

434 Aesch. *Agam.* 1291; *cf.* Hom. *Il.* 5.646, 9.313.

435 *cf.* my lecture *Dionysos und das Tragische in der Antigone* (Frankfurt a. M., 1935), 9 *f.*

436 A. Brelich, *Aspetti della morte nelle inscrizioni sepolcrali dell' impero Romano* (Budapest, 1937), 8.

437 Soph. 241d τὸ μὴ ὂν ἔστι κατά τι.

438 Theophr. *De sensu* 3.

439 Cited by Scheler from Frobenius.

440 *cf.* Soph. *Ant.* 809 *ff.*

441 F. Brunetière.

442 *Od.* 11.634–5; *pulchra Prosperpina* Verg. *Aen.* 6.142.

443 Lévy-Bruhl, *Les fonctions mentales dans les sociétés inférieurs* (Paris, 1922), 321.

444 S. Freud, *Beyond the Pleasure Principle* (Vol. 18 of the Standard Edition; London, 1955).

445 *Dionysos und das Tragische in der Antigone*, 13.

446 *cf.* my remarks in *Gnomon* 1933, 305 *f.*

447 *Dionysos und das Tragische in der Antigone*, 10.

448 *Theog.* 728.

ACKNOWLEDGMENTS

Alinari: 102, 105, 107–109, 113–115, 118–120, 123

Anderson, Rome: 17, 84, 94, 103, 106, 116, 117

By courtesy of the Trustees of the British Museum: 11, 12, 19, 25, 47, 49–56, 97

Ronald Doyle: 87

German Archaeological Institute, Rome: 82, 122, 124

Hirmer Verlag, Munich: 1, 4, 10, 13–16, 18, 20–23, 26–30, 32–43, 57–66, 70, 71, 83–85, 91–93, 95, 96, 98–101

S. Lang: 5–9

Musei Communali, Rome: 121

Rosmarie Pierer: 67–69, 86, 88–90

Josephine Powell: 2

H. Roger-Viollet: 24, 45, 48

Edwin Smith: 25, 56

Thames & Hudson archives: 81

V. & N. Tombazi, Athens: 3, 31, 46, 72–80

Vatican Museum: 110, 111

The publisher and the author are grateful to Professor Papadimitriou for his courtesy in providing the originals of Plates 3, 31, 46 and 72–80.

The publisher's and the author's thanks are also due to Professor H. Kähler for the loan of photographs for Plates 44, 102, 104, 109 and 112. These are taken from his *Rom und seine Welt* (Bayrischer Schulbuchverlag, Munich.)

Q*

INDEX